First published 1976 by
The Hamlyn Publishing Group Limited
London · New York · Sydney · Toronto
Astronaut House, Feltham, Middlesex, England
© The Hamlyn Publishing Group Limited 1976
ISBN 0 600 33977 7
Printed in Spain by Mateu-Cromo, S.A.

Contents

Acknowledgements

Alinari, Florence pages 76–77 bottom; Austrian Institute page 69; Austrian State Tourist Office page 28; Belgian National Office page 71 top; British Museum page 72; Camera Press (Jane Bown) page 66; J. Allan Cash page 71 bottom; Bruce Coleman Ltd. (F. Allan) page 53 and back cover, (Nelly Peter) page 67; Colour Library International page 65; Hamlyn Group Picture Library pages 15, 19, 23, 24, 27, 35 and 62; E. D. Lacey page 74; National Gallery, London pages 76–77 top; R. H. Parker page 75; John Ruler page 70; Sotheby's page 73; Syndication International page 78; Wales Tourist Board, Bwrdd Croeso Cymru, front cover.

Riding

with Elwyn Hartley Edwards

Illustrated by
John Lobban

Hamlyn
London · New York · Sydney · Toronto

Buying a Pony

Anyone can buy a pony so long as he has the money to pay for it! Indeed, in so far as one pays the purchase price and receives goods in exchange, it is not much different from buying a motor-car or a bicycle. To buy the *right* pony, however, is a very different matter, and since ponies are not lumps of metal with wheels attached, it is a good deal more complex.

On the other hand, if you use your common sense throughout there is no reason why you should not end up owning a completely suitable animal.

Opposite: are pictures of the nine British native pony breeds, all of which are first-rate riding ponies, as well as being tough, hardy and constitutionally sound. They are, (1) Connemara (2) Dale (3) Dartmoor (4) Exmoor (5) Fell (6) Highland (7) New Forest (8) Shetland and (9) Welsh Mountain.

Left: this is a high-class riding pony of good conformation. His general proportions are excellent and he has a particularly well-sloped riding shoulder which will ensure good action. On the other hand this sort of pony might not be ideal for a beginner.

How to keep him

Well before you get to the point of looking at ponies, I suggest that you should give a lot of thought to the subject of keeping one. You have to recognise that a pony is a continuing expense. He needs feeding and shoeing regularly,

for instance, and this costs money. It is no good saving up to buy a pony and then finding that you cannot afford to keep one.

What's more, a pony needs somewhere to live — a fenced paddock of suitable size (not less than half a hectare) which offers some form of shelter and can be provided with water easily. If you have such a paddock or can rent one there is no problem, but otherwise you will have to consider keeping him at livery. That means boarding the pony out at a convenient riding stable, which will then be responsible for his well-being. It is, however, the most expensive way of keeping him.

A suitable pony

Second, you must give some thought to the type of pony that will suit you best in size, temperament and ability.

Obviously you need a pony that is not too small or too big. If, when you are mounted, your feet hang about 30 cm below the girth, then the pony is too small. Since he has already reached his full size but you are still growing, matters will only get worse as time goes on. Conversely, if your feet reach only half-way down his sides, he will be too big until your legs grow longer. The ideal is that your feet should hang a little above the girth; but if anything, it is wiser to choose a pony a few centimetres bigger than you need rather than the other way about.

Much the most important factor, however, is that of temperament. Some ponies are naturally hot and excitable, although probably highly couraged; others are the opposite, quiet, lethargic and unambitious, whilst still more fall somewhere in between. Generally, it is best to avoid the extremes. But whatever sort of pony you choose, do make sure you are temperamentally suited to each other. If you are a nervous rider with little experience, go for the quieter, more solid pony who will give you confidence. When you have been riding for some time and have more confidence, then is the time to look round for something that will give you a brighter ride, and on which you will be able to go jumping or compete in hunter trials, and so on.

The ability of the pony has to be related to the work that is going to be expected of him. A hairy dobbin, for instance, however sweet and amiable, will not get very far if you are keen on jumping competitively or if you fancy trying your luck in the show ring. On the other hand, if you aspire to nothing more than hacking about and competing at a modest level then he will do well enough.

The sort to buy

One crucial factor in choosing a pony concerns the facilities you have for keeping him. If he is to live out in the paddock all the year round, he must be the sort that can take wintering-out in his stride. Most ponies will live out quite happily, but there are exceptions. Those with a lot of Thoroughbred or Arab blood in their make-up do not do so well living out, and some of them may need to be stabled in the winter or, at least, to be fitted with a New Zealand rug if they are not to become cold and miserable.

Without doubt the best types of all-round ponies in the world are those of the British native breeds or those closely related to them. There are, of course, other ponies in Europe, notably the Norwegian and Haflinger, that are equally hardy and tough. There are nine recognised breeds of British native pony. The bigger ones, going up to 14 h.h. and over, are the Highland, Fell and Dale, the larger of the Welsh Cobs, the New Forest and the Connemara, which originates on the West coast of Ireland. The smaller breeds are the Dartmoor and Exmoor, the Welsh Mountain pony and smaller Welsh Cob and the very tiny Shetland. There is, however, a category of Welsh pony, called Section B, which stands up to 13·2 h.h. and is probably the finest riding pony to be found anywhere, having quality, beautiful freedom of pace and yet retaining the characteristic toughness of the native breeds.

Many ponies, of course, will not be pure-breds of any one of these breeds but will be the result of cross-breeding. None the less, the majority, at any rate in Britain, will carry some percentage of native blood.

Conformation

When people are talking about ponies and horses, you will frequently hear the word 'conformation' used. You should understand what this means and why it is important that any pony or horse should have 'good conformation'.

The word refers to the overall physical shape of the pony. In very simple terms, a pony of 'good' conformation is one whose individual parts: head, neck, quarters, back and limbs, are all in proportion to each other. If, for instance, a pony has a very large head it will be out of proportion to the rest of his body, as will a pair of weak-looking hind legs or a very long back. But, you may ask, why is all this so important? Well, let us take the three examples given: the large head, the poor quarters and the long back. In the first case, a large head will upset the balance of the pony, he will carry it low and so put most of his weight on the forehand, that means the part of his body in front of his withers. As a result he will not be able to move so freely and he will always hang very heavily on your hands. Poor, weak quarters will also affect his performance seriously. The power house of the pony lies in his quarters, which push him forward. If they are strong and well-formed, he will have the necessary power to gallop and jump; if they are not, he will be that much less efficient. And what about the long back? This is really a very important part of the pony because it is here that the weight of the rider is carried. Obviously, a short, deep structure is needed in this area if the pony is to be able to carry weight without discomfort. A long back must necessarily be a weak one, too.

So it is better to buy as well-made a pony as you can find, for the good reason that he will be able to do his work better and with less risk of straining any part of his body.

Below: this is exactly the type of pony to be avoided. He is out of proportion and looks weak in all departments. His shoulder is upright and his head and neck so badly set on that it will be impossible for him to give a good ride. His middle is about as poor as it could be and there is no evidence of strength in those badly shaped quarters. This pony would stand no chance in the show ring, nor would he perform well at anything else.

Compare the diagrams of the pony of good conformation with those of the badly-made pony, and it is clear what I mean. There is also a diagram of 'the proportionate horse'. Frankly, this is the ideal, and you will never find it completely realised, but it is a good guide and you can have a lot of fun comparing the measurements of your own pony with those given in the diagram.

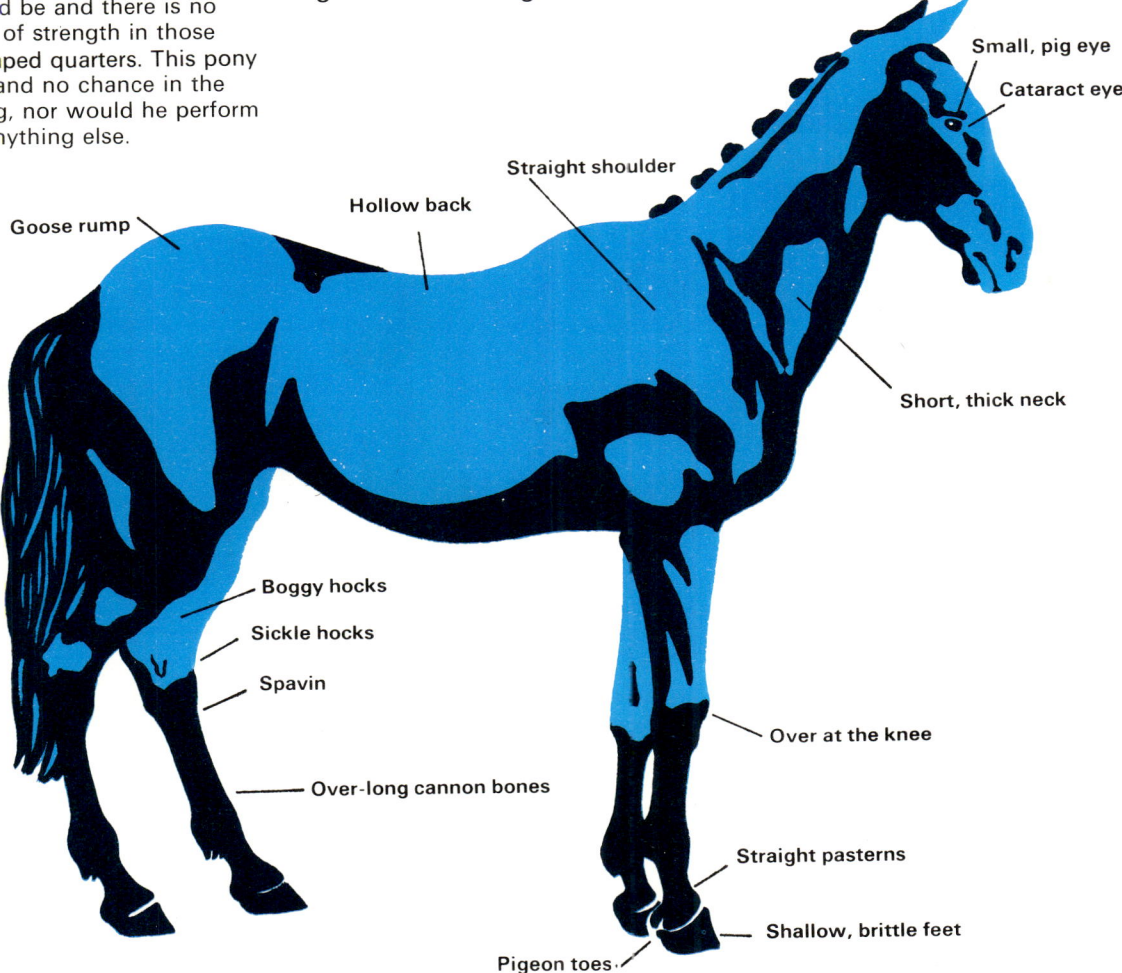

- Goose rump
- Hollow back
- Straight shoulder
- Small, pig eye
- Cataract eye
- Short, thick neck
- Boggy hocks
- Sickle hocks
- Spavin
- Over-long cannon bones
- Over at the knee
- Straight pasterns
- Shallow, brittle feet
- Pigeon toes

There is, however, a lot more to assessing the conformation of a horse or pony than has been mentioned so far. Indeed, to assess the finer points of conformation you need a lot of knowledge and experience. Before you start looking at ponies with a view to buying one, study the pictures of winning ponies which are to be found in the magazines. This will give you some idea of the make and shape you should be looking for. If you can also go to a few horse shows and watch ponies being judged you will learn even more about conformation.

Here, however, are a few tips which should help you.

To start with, stand well back and take a long look at the pony as a whole. This should tell you whether he is fairly well-made or hopelessly out of proportion. Compare him, in fact, with the pictures of good ponies that you have seen.

Now, look at him in more detail, starting with his *head*. It should be neat and fine, not coarse and heavy; the ears

should be pricked and alert and, above all, the eye should be big and calm. Small, piggy eyes, often showing a lot of white, are a pretty fair indication of bad temper, particularly if they are accompanied by laid-back ears. The head itself should sit nicely on to the *neck*. It should not be carried too high nor too low. In either of those cases, bitting and control will be made more difficult.

The neck itself needs to be reasonably long and slim and slightly curved on the top. A neck set on 'upside-down', concave on the top and with a pronounced bulge on the under side, is called a 'ewe-neck' and it makes life very uncomfortable for the rider, who will find control difficult and will also be risking a bump on the nose. Very short, very thick necks are almost as bad. Ponies with these are often called 'strong', which really means that you cannot stop them!

Now pass to the withers, the bony projection at the base of the neck. Ponies do not have such clearly defined withers as horses, but very flat ones should be avoided. They make it difficult to keep a saddle in place and they usually go with straight, upright shoulders. You will hear a lot of talk about *shoulders*, and, indeed, their shape is very important. A good shoulder is one that is long and well-sloped with the forelegs placed rather more forward than to the rear. Such a shoulder allows the pony to stretch out and make full use of his forelegs, whilst the opposite sort results in a short up and down stride, particularly when the forelegs are placed well back. As well as being uncomfortable, this up and down action is wasteful, as it does not allow the leg to cover much ground, and it also causes far more jarring to the limb as the foot meets the ground. It is this sort of concussion, particularly when ponies are trotted on roads or hard ground, that can cause leg troubles that may make the pony lame.

You should now let your eye pass down the forelegs, which should be an exact pair, with feet of the same size and not turned in or out. You want a strong, muscular forearm (the piece above the *knee*) whilst the knee itself should be big and flat. Under the knee is the *cannon bone*, which needs to be short and straight: short, because, just like the back, that makes for strength. Long cannon bones are weak ones and cause trouble. When we talk about a horse or pony having 'good bone' or 'plenty of bone' we do not mean that they have long legs. We are referring to the measurement round the leg taken below the knee. Twenty centimetres of bone is considered to be very adequate. Some ponies will not have as much as this but pony bone is usually very dense in its structure, which gives it great strength and allows the pony to carry weight that may often be out of proportion to its size.

Bad faults in the forelegs are when the leg is 'tied in below the knee', when the measurement round the cannon below the knee is less than one taken lower down near the fetlock joint. This is a serious weakness and nearly always leads to lameness in the end. The other bad fault is when the cannon, instead of being straight, curves inwards. This is called 'back at the knee'.

Above: two examples of neck conformation – the top one is somewhat 'cresty' but is preferable to the one below which has no top line and is joined to a rather straight shoulder. The picture of the leg shows a good, straight limb, with a short cannon and well-formed foot.

The *fetlock* does not want to be round like an apple but hard and flat. Swelling or puffiness in this joint usually indicates that the pony has done a lot of hard work — too much, in fact. Below the fetlock is the *pastern*, which is really a shock-absorber for the leg. If it is short and upright it will not be able to do its job properly, and so it should be fairly well-sloped, but not too much so, otherwise it will put too much strain on the tendons and ligaments which run down the back of the leg.

Napoleon used to say that 'armies march on their stomachs'. That may be so, but horses and ponies walk, trot, canter or gallop on their *feet*, and unless these are well made and well-cared-for the animal will not be much use.

If you look at the feet, you should see deep, open heels, not nasty contracted ones, and a good big frog, which is the principal shock-absorber. The sole should be slightly concave, not flat which would make it more susceptible to injury from rough going.

Before leaving the forehand, take a look at the *chest*. It has to be wide enough to allow the lungs to expand. If it is too narrow with the forelegs too close together, 'both coming out of the same hole', the pony will not be able to use his lungs properly.

The middle piece of the pony, to tie up with a fair breadth of chest, must have a 'deep girth'; deep, that is, from a point just behind the withers to one just behind the forelegs. It needs to be well rounded, the ribs sprung outwards, without a flat-sided appearance.

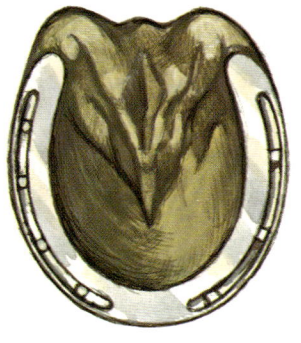

Above: is a nicely formed leg with a flat, not round, fetlock joint. Also, a foot as it should be, open and with a well-defined frog.

Right: the table below illustrates an easy and approximate way to measure a perfectly proportioned horse. Taking the head as a basis for measurement (A), the length between the points listed should be equal to each other. The measurements for (B) are also equal.

A = 1 length of head, 2 point of hock to ground, 3 point of hock to fold of stifle, 4 chestnut to base of foot, 5 depth of body at girth, 6 fold of stifle to croup, 7 posterior angle of scapula to point of hip. Length from point of shoulder to seat bone = 2½ times length of head. Height from fetlock to elbow = approximately height of elbow—wither. B = 1 seat bone—point of hip, 2 seat bone—stifle, 3 stifle to point of hip. A line dropped from the seat bone meets the point of the hock and continues down the back of the cannon bone.

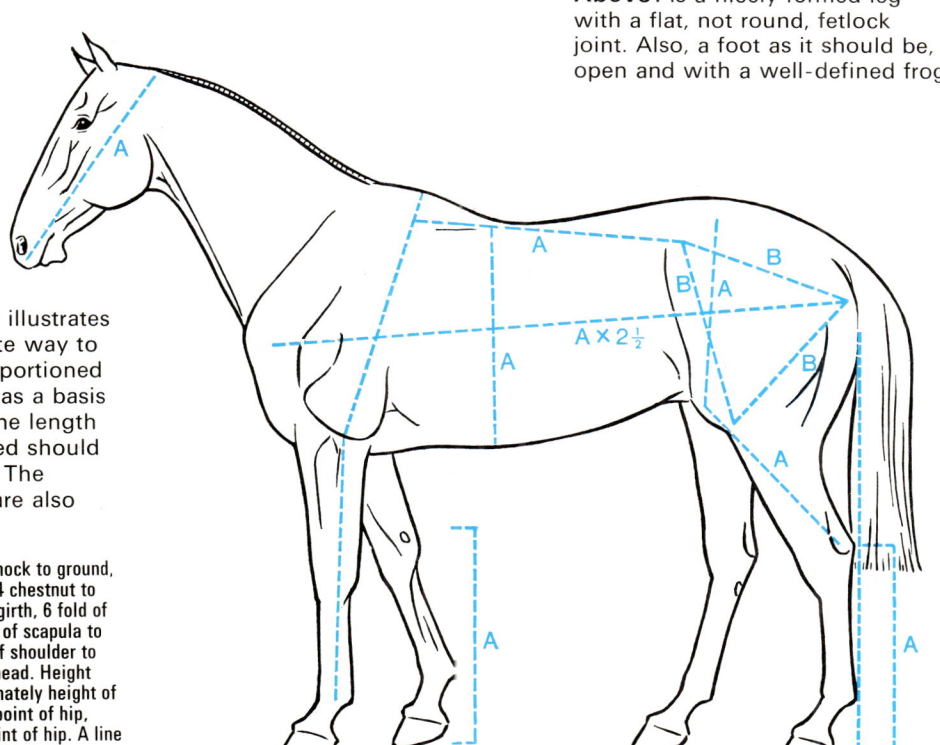

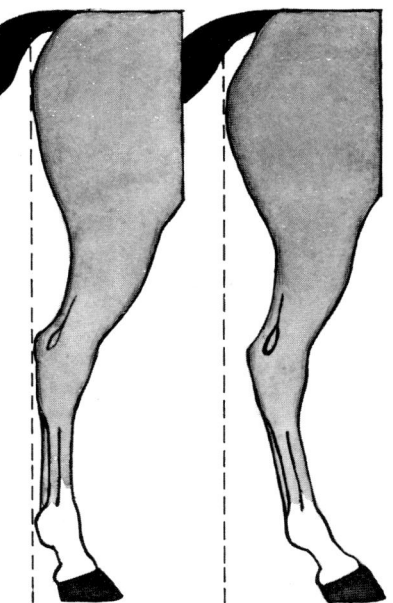

Above: on the left is a good straight hind-leg. The one on the right is an example of a weak sickle hock.

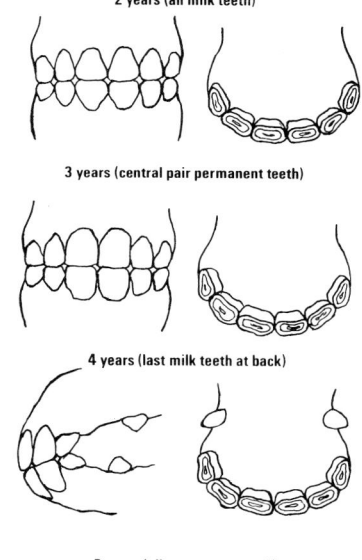

2 years (all milk teeth)

3 years (central pair permanent teeth)

4 years (last milk teeth at back)

5 years (all permanent teeth)

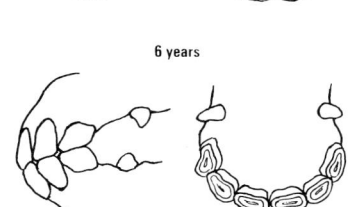

6 years

Ponies with hollow *backs* and the opposite, roach backs, are to be avoided, they cannot carry a saddle properly.

Finally, the pony needs a set of good, strong quarters. Quarters that slope down with the tail set low are weak. The hindlegs must also look strong and be very well developed in the 'second thigh', or gaskin, the area between the stifle and the hock joint. A good way to judge the excellence or otherwise of a hindleg is to imagine a line drawn to the ground from the point of the buttock. That line should meet the point of the hock and follow the line of cannon bone. Hocks carried well in front of the line and overbent are called 'sickle hocks', and since they cause more strain on joints and ligaments, (ligaments are made of hard fibres which are attached to bones to hold them in place) are bad. Hocks carried behind the imaginary line also cause more strain, and are not able to propel the horse forward so effectively.

Age

How old should the pony be? Within reason it does not matter. Young ponies of four or even five years will not have had time to learn very much, and so, unless you are pretty experienced and are able to school a pony, they are best avoided. *Do not buy* a pony under four years of age. Young ponies, babies really, of two and three years are not ready to be ridden and it is cruel to use them. Their bodies and their bones are not developed, nor are their little minds. If they are made to carry weight at this age, a great deal of stress and strain is put on their limbs, which can, indeed, become deformed. You are, in fact, preventing them from growing up naturally. You would not be asked by your parents to carry heavy bags of coal about, nor would your father expect you to be able to give him a piggy-back for a couple of kilometres a day. When you ride a young pony before he is strong enough to carry you, you are being less than reasonable. What is more, since he is so young, the pony will not understand what is wanted and because he is sore and stiff he can quickly become sour and bad-tempered.

Left & below: expert horsemen tell the age of a horse from the appearance of the teeth. Up to the age of five the pony is shedding milk teeth and replacing them with permanent ones. At four, male horses grow 'tushes' behind the incisor teeth. At nine all horses develop a groove (Galvayne's groove) on the corner teeth and this grows downwards, until at the age of 20 years, it has reached the bottom of the tooth.

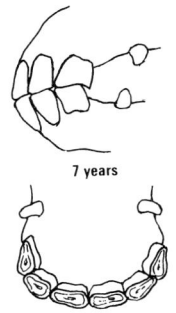

7 years

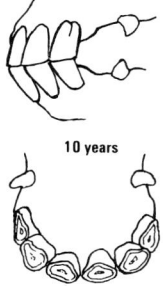

10 years

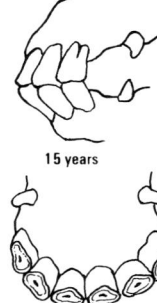

15 years

Very old ponies are not suitable either, for obvious reasons. Probably something between 6–10 years is ideal, but do not discard the pony that is a bit older than that if he is otherwise sound and healthy.

Male or female?

Whether a pony is male (a gelding) or female (a mare) may not be too important. Mares, particularly in the breeding season, can be a bit touchy and flighty, but this does not apply to all of them by any means. Geldings, who are not affected by the breeding season, are usually, but not always, more even-tempered. Generally speaking it all depends on the individual.

Colour

This does not matter either, so long as the colour is a good strong one and not wishy-washy. The latter tend to be less tough constitutionally. Chestnuts have a reputation for being 'hot' and excitable, and indeed some of them are, particularly the mares, but you should remember the old saying 'a good horse is never a bad colour'.

Where to buy

Ponies can be bought from a variety of sources. You can go to a sale and buy whatever catches your eye, but I do not advise you to do so unless you and your parents are very knowledgeable indeed. There is little opportunity to find out much about a pony at a sale and probably no chance to give him a trial. For these reasons a sale is probably the easiest way to buy a really unsuitable pony.

Above: 'a good horse is never a bad colour'.

1 Muzzle
2 Chin groove (or curb groove)
3 Bars of jaw
4 Throat (gullet)
5 Point of shoulder
6 Breast
7 Forearm
8 Elbow
9 Knee
10 Cannon bone
11 Fetlock joint
12 Pastern
13 Tendons
14 Girth
15 Base of neck
16 Ribs
17 Belly
18 Barrel
19 Sheath
20 Stifle
21 Shin
22 Chestnut
23 Coronet
24 Hoof (wall of foot)
25 Heel
26 Ergot
27 Fetlock
28 Back tendons
29 Shank
30 Seat of curb
31 Hock
32 Point of hock
33 Gaskin (second thigh)
34 Buttocks
35 Point of buttocks (seat-bone)
36 Dock
37 Hip joint
38 Thigh
39 Quarter
40 Croup
41 Point of croup
42 Point of hip (haunch bone or angle of haunch)
43 Flank
44 Back (saddle)
45 Withers
46 Crest
47 Poll
48 Loins

Below: the points of the horse.

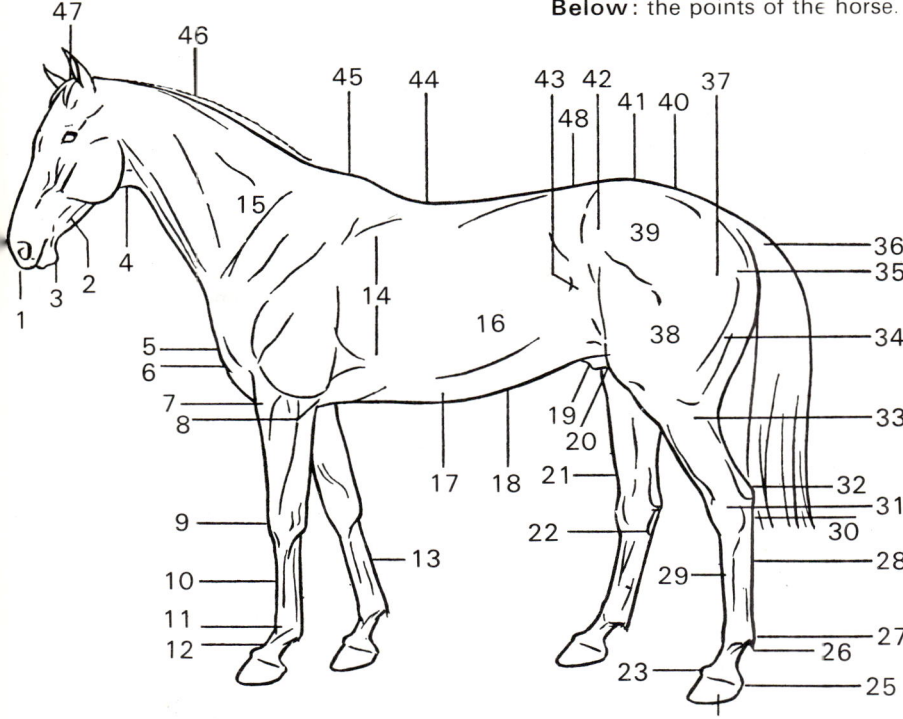

Above: make sure the horse you choose is easy to catch and box.

Below: before buying a pony make sure that he is easy to handle and never buy until he has been passed as sound by a veterinary surgeon.

In most areas there are dealers, who sell ponies and horses just as a butcher sells meat or a garage sells cars. They are just as much business men, and just as honest, as anyone else who makes a living by buying and selling and it would do their reputation no good at all to sell you a bad pony. There are, of course, 'back-yard' dealers who are not nearly so reputable, but to buy from an established horse-dealer is quite safe and satisfactory.

Many riding schools have animals for sale or will be prepared to find a suitable pony for a client. If you attend a school regularly, this is probably a good way to buy since the proprietor will know what sort of pony would suit you best. Lastly, you can buy privately, from people who will usually advertise what they have to sell in the magazines or in the local papers.

How to buy

From whatever source you decide to buy a pony it is always advisable to take somebody with you who knows about horses and is experienced. It could be someone you know in your area or the proprietor of your riding school, but *not* a teenage girl who knows it all — she doesn't.

When you have looked at the pony, having studied this chapter very carefully and made mother and father read it, too, watch the pony being trotted out. He should trot out gaily and freely and when he walks take good long strides, not short, pottery ones. Then get the owner to ride him and again watch carefully. Does he move away willingly without trying to get back to the gate? If all goes well, try him yourself and find out if he goes on when he is asked and whether he slows down obediently. Give him a little jump if you like so that you get the feel of him. If you like him, and it is no good if you do not, insist on taking him out on the roads to make sure he is safe in traffic. A traffic-shy pony is no good at all. When you get him back, handle him all over, picking up his feet and so on, and unsaddle him. Take your time about it all, after all you are the buyer.

Try to find out whether he is easy to box and catch. If he has allowed you to handle his feet he should be all right to shoe.

Now go away and think about it. If you still want the pony the next day, then ring up and say that you will buy him *subject to a veterinary inspection*. Do not be put off by people who say that he has just been vetted but insist on getting your own vet., or at any rate an independent one, to carry out the examination. If the vet. pronounces him sound in every respect then go ahead and buy. Never buy an unsound pony. However cheap, they are always the most expensive in the long run.

Buying `Tack`

Once you have acquired a pony you, and he, will need a certain amount of 'tack', which is a name given to saddlery. Riding ponies do not have 'harness' — that is the word used to describe the equipment of the driving horse.

As a minimum you will need a halter or headcollar, and a lead rope to lead him to and from his field and for tying him up. For riding, you will need a saddle, mounted with leathers, irons and a girth, plus, of course, a bridle.

You can buy very smart leather headcollars fitted with brass buckles. They look well, last a long time if they are properly looked after, but they are pretty expensive. A halter, made of jute, may not look quite so good, although they can be bought in a variety of colours, but they are made with a lead rope already attached and they are much cheaper and just as effective. If it is possible, the best sort to get is the type that is called a Yorkshire halter. This is the one which is fitted with a string throatlatch which will prevent it being pulled across an eye when in use.

Your saddle is a most important piece of equipment — far more important than you think. Properly designed and fitted it will be comfortable for both you and the pony, and it will really help you to sit correctly and securely — something which is just as much a benefit to the pony as to yourself. If you are sitting on a saddle that forces you to sit at the back, and on which you find it difficult to sit still, it will not add to the pony's comfort or to his ability to carry you well.

What sort of saddle should you buy? Always, in my opinion, one of modern design. It should be of the type that has a fairly pronounced dip to the seat, with a leather panel into which is built a knee roll. It does not need to be cut forward in an exaggerated way. Some jumping saddles are cut with a very forward flap and panel but, on ponies particularly, they can come too much on the shoulder and

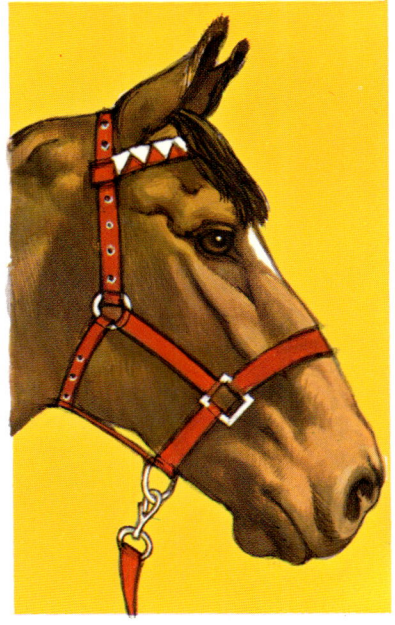

Above: this pony is wearing a rather 'flashy' headcollar. It isn't necessary to have a headcollar as extravagant as this one, but some sort of headcollar or halter is essential.

Below: your saddle is a most important piece of equipment. If it is well designed, like the one this man is riding in, it will help you to sit correctly.

prevent the pony moving freely. Choose instead what the saddlers call a general or all-purpose saddle, where the flap is not so far inclined forward.

The advantages of this type of saddle are many. First, the rider is almost compelled to sit into the centre of the saddle. He or she needs to sit centrally for the very good reason that it places the body as nearly as possible over the pony's point of balance, or centre of gravity, whichever you prefer. Perhaps that needs some explanation.

Think first of a simple see-saw which is balanced on its centre. If you were to sit directly over the point of balance you would experience very little movement as the see-saw went up and down. On the other hand, if you sat at the end of the see-saw, as is usual, your body moves in quite a large arc. A pony is not dissimilar, and if you sit as nearly as you can over his centre of balance, which we will look at in a moment, that will be the place where you will feel the least of the movement. If, for instance, you sat on his rump you would, as on the see-saw, find yourself feeling the movement very much more. That is one reason why your saddle should encourage you to sit centrally. If it had a flat, rather than a dipped seat and was, perhaps, higher in front than behind, you would sit nearer the cantle and nearer, therefore, to the strong movement of the quarters which would not be nearly so comfortable or secure.

In the pony, the point of balance is not, in fact, in the dead centre of his body. Because of the weight of the head and neck, the centre of balance in a pony is further forward, in fact, if you look at the diagram you will see that it is at the junction of two imaginary lines, one drawn vertically through a point some 20 cm behind the withers and the other drawn horizontally through the shoulder. There, right in the centre of his body, is his point of balance, and over that point is where you must try to sit. That, of course, is easy enough when the pony is standing still, but when he moves at faster paces, such as the canter, and even more so when he gallops and jumps, he stretches his neck out, puts more weight on the

Below: this is a saddle of modern design that is not made with an exaggerated forward flap. It is called a 'general-purpose' saddle and is built with a dipped seat, which helps you to sit centrally, and is fitted with a panel which incorporates a knee roll to give greater security. The panel, seen as a whole in the diagram on the right of the picture, acts as a cushion between the pony's back and the wooden 'tree' on which the saddle is built. It is made, as it were, in two halves, separated by a 'channel'. This channel ensures that there is no pressure on the pony's backbone. In the centre diagram are the girth straps, which are fitted with an oblong piece of leather. This is called a girth 'safe' or 'guard' and is pulled down over the girth buckles so that they do not rub holes in the saddle flap.

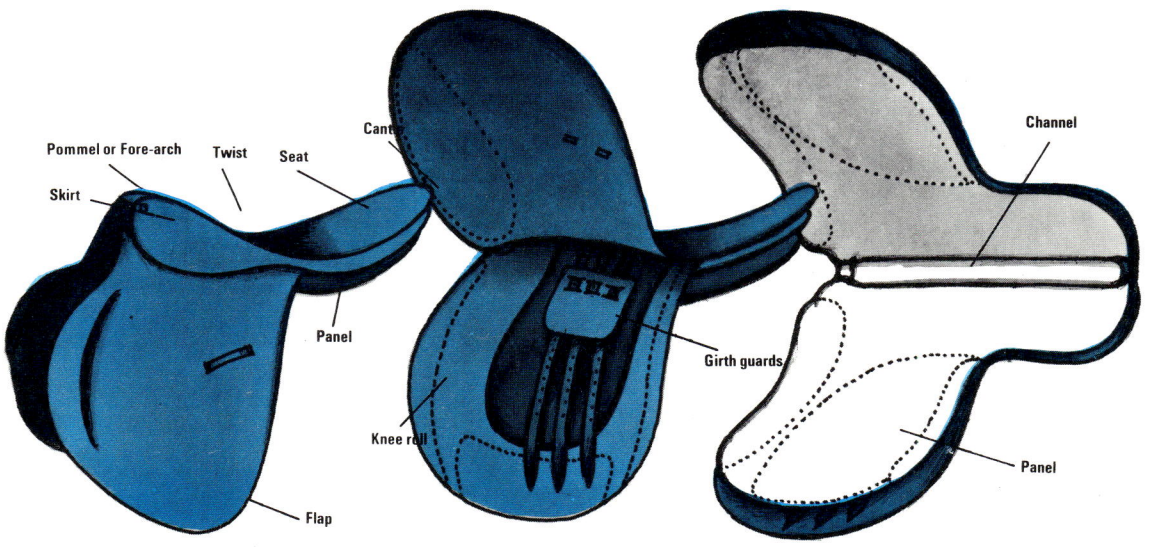

Pommel or Fore-arch · Twist · Seat · Cantle · Channel · Skirt · Panel · Knee roll · Girth guards · Panel · Flap

front end and so his centre of balance moves further forward. In order to keep your body in line with his centre you then have to move your weight forward.

To be able to do so, particularly when jumping, you need a saddle that is going to help you, not one that makes everything more difficult. Since the position of your legs has a considerable effect on your seat and trunk you need a little help there, also. In the modern saddle, you sit in the deepest part, which is also the narrowest, and your legs are helped to stay in position by the presence of the knee rolls. In fact 'knee' is not really the correct description for these rolls as it is really to the part of the thigh just above the knee that they give support. To complete the rider's comfort, and therefore his security, the modern saddle has very little bulk under the flap, allowing the rider's legs to be in close contact with the pony.

But how does all this affect the pony, whose comfort is even more important than yours? The answer is that the saddle, constructed as described, by positioning the rider correctly assists the pony to carry the weight more easily. If the weight were carried well behind the pony's centre of balance, it would over-burden his quarters and prevent them

Below: this diagram shows the saddle fitted in relation to the pony's point of balance, which is at the intersection of the two broken lines. The object of the well-designed modern saddle is to position the rider as nearly as possible over this point and to help her maintain this position without making any huge physical effort. It is easy to see that if the saddle seat was flat and the pommel (the front arch) higher than the back of the saddle (the cantle) the rider would be placed, automatically, well behind the point of balance and behind the movement of the pony, and there would be very little she could do about it. Riding in this position her weight would be carried too much on the quarters and would prevent the pony moving freely.

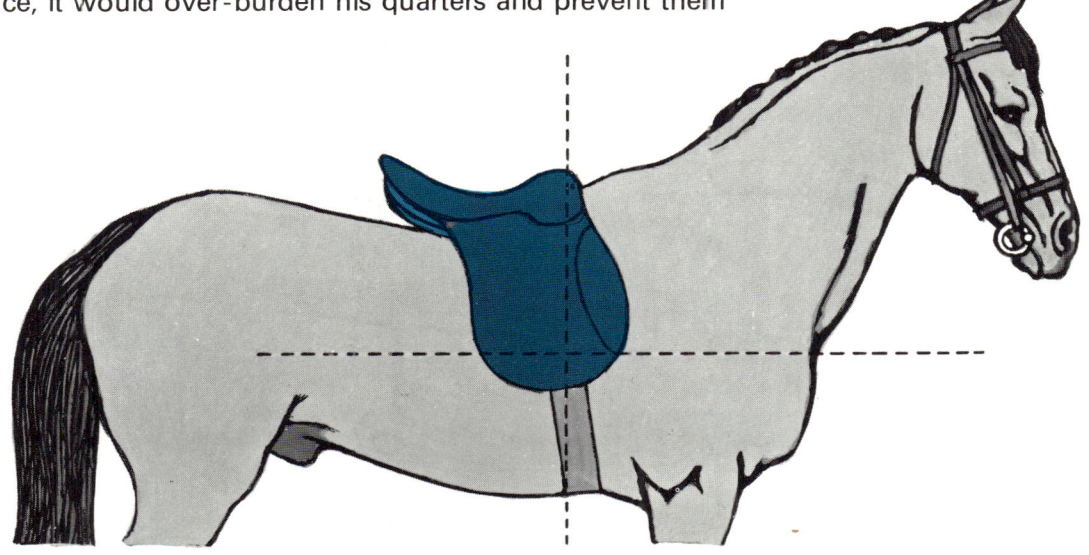

moving with their full freedom. Similarly, of course, if the rider perched *too* far forward, the forehand would be over-loaded, and again the pony would find it difficult to move freely. Finally, if we have a rider who, because of his saddle or for any other reason, is continually shifting his weight from back to front his actions will be continually upsetting the pony's balance, which is tiring for him and once more prevents the pony from moving as efficiently as he could or ought.

Saddle fitting

However well-designed a saddle may be it will do nothing but harm if it does not fit the pony as well as your shoes fit your feet.

It is always advisable when buying a saddle to have the saddler come out and fit it for you to the pony's back. Even so, you should know the main points of saddle fitting.

These are:

1. The saddle must lie level on the back, allowing the spine complete freedom along its whole length and breadth. In practice you need to be able to insert at least two fingers between the front arch, the pommel, and the pony's withers when you are mounted. The saddle must not touch the backbone at the cantle nor at any point between the latter and the pommel. If you stand behind the pony you should be able to see daylight right along the length of the saddle from back to front. The importance of the channel, dividing the two halves of the panel, is very great. It must at all times be well open. If it starts to close, pressure is put on the sides of the vertebrae making up the backbone. It follows that the panel must be sufficiently well-stuffed to hold the saddle above the spine.

2. The weight of the rider must be distributed evenly over the whole bearing surface of the saddle panel. This means that both sides of the panel must be stuffed

Below: if you stand behind the pony you should be able to see daylight right along the length of the saddle. The front of the saddle, at the pommel, should allow the insertion of two fingers between withers and front arch.

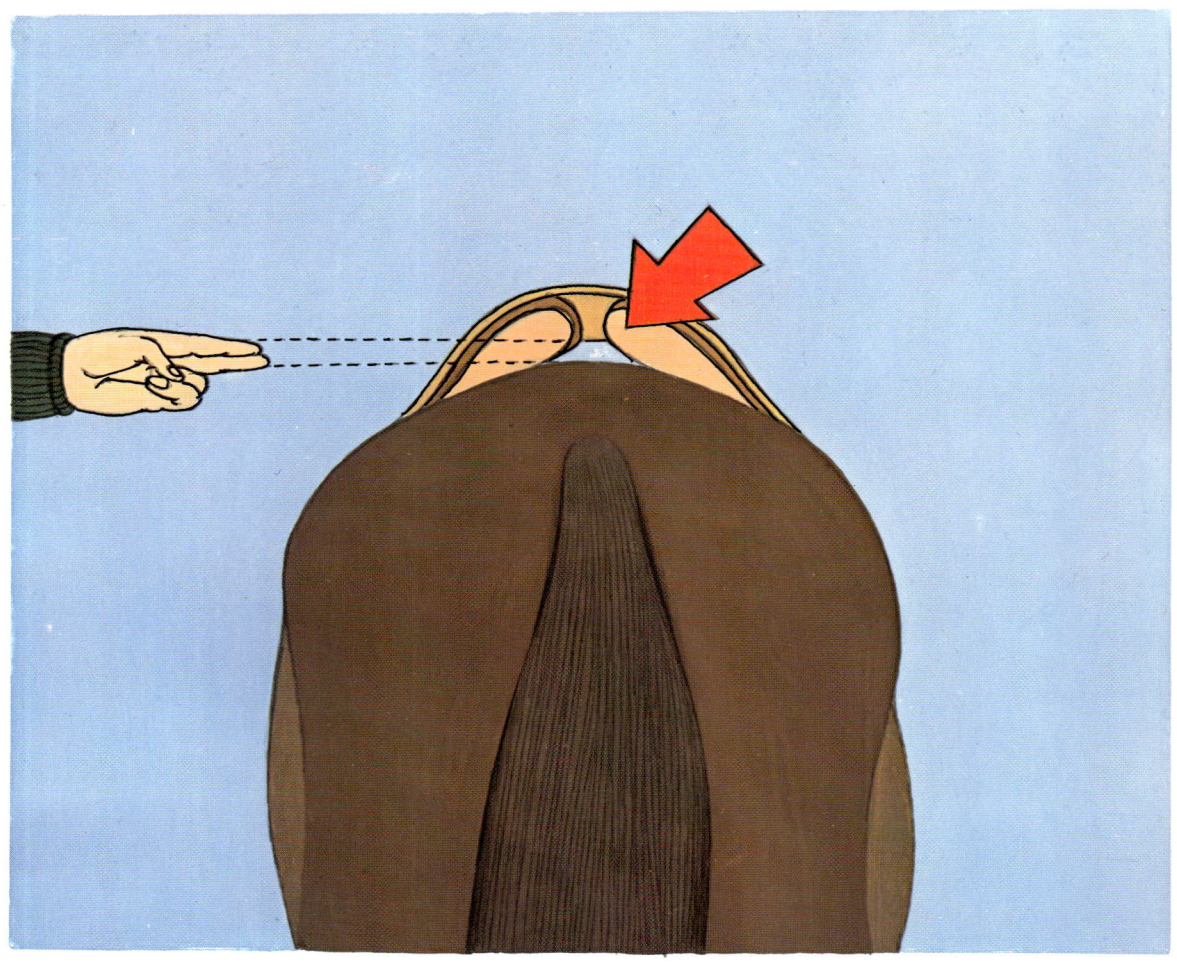

equally, otherwise more weight will be taken on one side than the other. The weight is, in fact, carried on the big muscles on the side of the spine.

3. The panel of the saddle must be reasonably soft and have no lumps that could cause points of pressure. It must, also, be clean!

4. Finally, no saddle is any good if its tree, the wooden foundation on which it is built, does not fit the pony's back right from the start. If the tree does not fit, neither will the saddle, however much the panel stuffing is adjusted. The tree, as you will see from the diagram, is composed of a rigid front arch on to which is joined the bars forming the seat. The stirrup bars are attached to the ends of the front arch, which are called the 'points'. The front arch of the tree has to conform to the shape of the back over the withers and it is usually made in narrow, medium and broad fittings. Ponies usually require the latter. If the shape of the front arch is too narrow, the saddle will certainly clear the top of the withers but the points will undoubtedly press into the pony some 8–10 cm below and on either side of the withers. Conversely, if the tree is too wide there will not be clearance between the pommel and the withers.

If we neglect these elementary rules the saddle may cause sores or, at best, discomfort. Saddle sores are caused by pressure or by friction and they occur most commonly on the withers, but even a lump in a panel can cause a nasty gall. Should the saddle pinch or press on the backbone when the pony is moving, it will cause him much the same discomfort as you would experience if your shoes were too tight. A

Above: here the rider is sitting comfortably in a well-fitting modern saddle that will give her the maximum amount of help in maintaining her seat. Because the saddle fits well and positions the rider centrally it will also help the horse to give of his best.

normally willing pony can often become sour, playing up and even refusing to jump, just because his saddle is hurting him, and it is not surprising. You can well understand that if a pony gets his back hurt every time he jumps, he will soon come to the conclusion that he is better off keeping all four feet on the ground.

Girths, leathers and irons

The cheapest girth and one which is as satisfactory as any, is one made of nylon cord. But you can, if you wish, go in for a leather girth, like the Balding pattern, which is cut away at the elbow so as to reduce the risk of chafing. The thing to remember when buying a girth is to get one of the correct length. It should be long enough so that the buckles, when the girth is done up, lie just behind the bend in your knee. Some ponies carry a saddle better if they wear a Twin girth which has a centre of pimple rubber, which gives a good grip on the belly. Whatever sort of girth you buy, make sure your saddle is fitted with a pair of girth guards slid on to the girth straps. These pieces of soft leather stop the buckles from coming into contact with the flaps and cutting holes in them.

Choose fairly narrow leathers, no more than 2·5 cm wide, so that they are not too bulky, and since all stirrup leathers stretch a little in use, remember to change them from side to side so that they will stretch evenly — most riders, although they ought not, tend to put more weight on one iron than the other.

Your stirrup irons, on the other hand, need to be roomy and heavy, so that should you fall your foot will come free at once. If you like, you can buy rubber stirrup treads to slot into the foot of the iron. They help to keep your foot in place and they also keep your feet warm in cold weather.

Numnahs made of sheepskin, or plastic foam covered with linen, are rarely necessary for a pony. If the saddle fits you don't really need one, except in exceptional cases. Indeed, they can be more trouble than they are worth, particularly the sheepskin variety. Firstly, they put you further away from the pony; secondly, they make the pony's back very hot, which can in itself cause soreness, and lastly, they get very dirty and so need constant washing.

Lots of people, however, like to use a saddle cloth to save the panel of the saddle from getting dirty. If you do use one, however, you must make sure it is tucked well up into the front arch, otherwise it can stretch tightly across the withers and cause soreness.

The bridle

There are all sorts of bridles, but it is my advice that you should use the simplest possible. The basic bridle is the *snaffle* with either a jointed bit or one with a half-moon, or mullen, mouth. The latter is the mildest of all and is usually made from either rubber, nylon or vulcanite. A complete

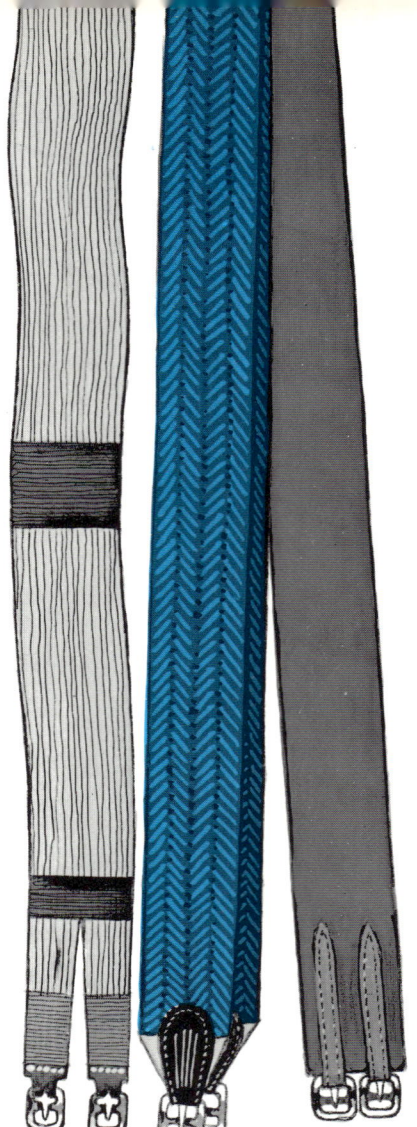

Above: these are three types of girth in common use. Left to right, a nylon girth, a pair of web girths and a girth of soft folded leather.

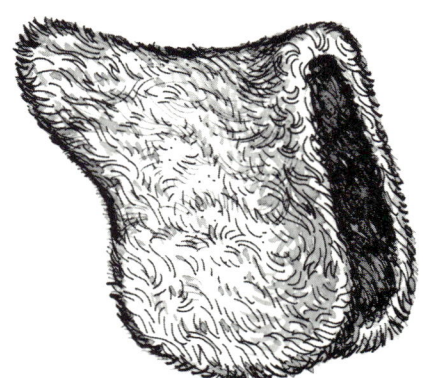

Above: a sheepskin numnah. Numnahs are occasionally necessary but are rarely needed for ponies. 'If the saddle fits you don't really need one.'

snaffle bridle consists of a headpiece in which is incorporated the throatlatch, a browband, two cheek-pieces, the bit, a pair of reins, and a simple cavesson noseband. However, for ponies that are a little strong, a drop noseband can be substituted for the cavesson type. The nosepiece of the drop noseband is fitted lower than the cavesson noseband, about 7 cm above the nostrils, with the back strap encircling the lower jaw by being fastened under the bit. This device closes the mouth and stops the pony from sliding the bit to one side. It also puts pressure on the nose so bringing the head down and giving the rider more control.

Another bridle used for strong ponies is that using a Kimblewick bit, which again lowers the head and because of the port (the bump in the centre of the mouthpiece) removes pressure from the tongue and transfers it directly to the bars of the mouth. The 'bars' are those areas of gum between the front (incisor) teeth and the back (molar) teeth. In addition, more control is gained by the use of a curb chain, acting on the curb groove of the lower jaw.

The Pelham is a near relation of the Kimblewick but in this case two reins are fitted. The top, *bradoon* or snaffle, rein, acts in the same way as an ordinary snaffle, whereas the use of the lower, *curb*, rein causes a stronger, downward pressure of the mouthpiece across the tongue and bars and also brings the curb chain into play. Many ponies go well in a Pelham but there is no point in using one if your pony goes just as well in a snaffle. It is possible to use a Pelham with a single rein by employing a leather rounding to join the bradoon and curb rings, but then you might as well use a Kimblewick.

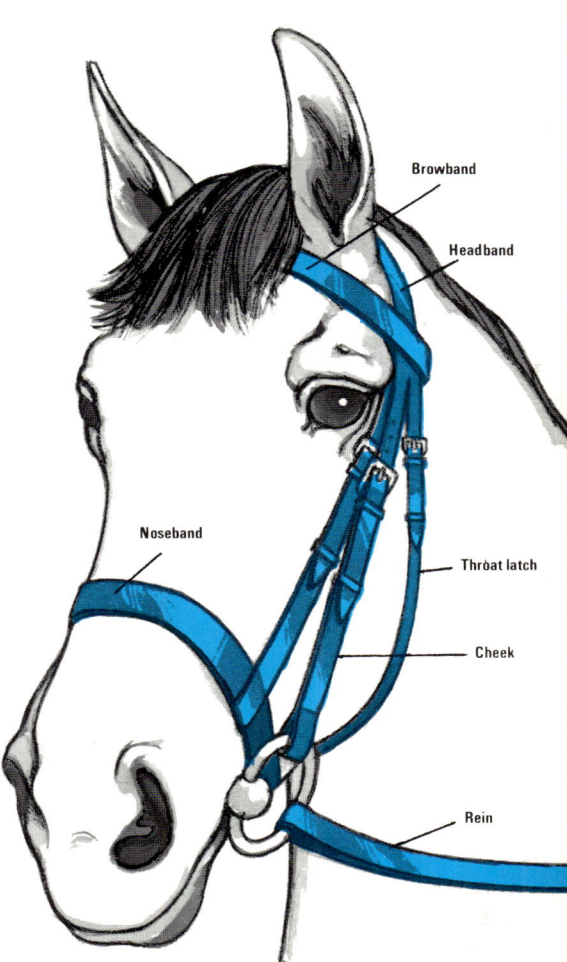

Above: a plain snaffle bridle.

Left: the far bit is a half-moon or 'mullen' mouth snaffle and the near, a mullen mouth Pelham. Both mouthpieces are made from either vulcanite or nylon.

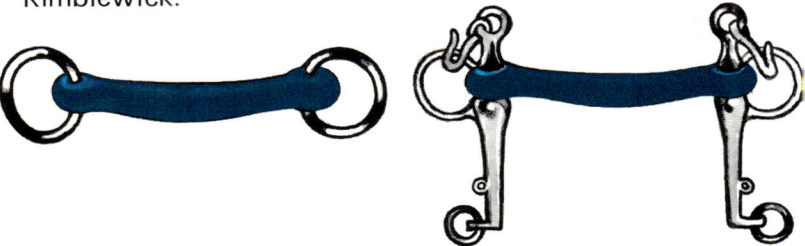

Reins are made in great variety. Apart from the plain leather rein, you can buy them made of plaited nylon, plaited or laced leather, and those covered with a rubber hand part. All these variations are designed to give a better grip, particularly in wet weather.

For showing in the ring, ponies are normally expected, at any rate in British show classes, to wear a double or Weymouth bridle which consists of two separate bits — on the top the snaffle or bradoon and below it the curb bit. This, however, is the bridle for the schooled and educated pony and the rider who has attained a similar standard. Until you are really a good rider it is best left alone.

Fitting the bridle

When the bridle is in position the bit should be wide enough to project a little on either side of the mouth and should be placed just high enough in the mouth to cause a slight wrinkling of the lips. With a cavesson noseband it should be possible to insert two fingers between it and the jawbones when it is fastened. The throatlatch should be fastened loosely enough to allow three fingers between it and the throat. If it is too tight you throttle the pony and prevent him flexing his head. Particular attention must be paid to the browband. If it is too short it will cause the headpiece to be pulled up against the ears, and this will cause the pony discomfort and result in head shaking. He cannot concentrate on his work if he is not comfortable, and complete comfort is what we should aim at when fitting any article of saddlery.

Martingales

Martingales are used, primarily, to control the position of the head and to make the action of the bit more effective. There are two main types: the standing and the running. The former is fastened to the back of the cavesson noseband, never to a drop which would be unduly severe, in order to prevent the horse carrying or throwing his head too high. It acts, therefore, on the nose. The running variety fastens to the reins and causes a lowering of the head by acting directly on the mouth. Both give greater control over an impetuous, tearaway type, but both are often used for no good reason and, in general, it is better to save your money and do without them.

If you must use one or the other, adjust them so that the top of the standing or the rings of the running are on a level with the withers.

Above: here the bit is being inserted gently into the pony's mouth with the left hand whilst the right, held at the poll, draws the bridle upwards.

Below: the pony on the left is wearing a running martingale, fastened to the reins and so acting on the mouth. The other pony has a standing martingale fastened to his noseband.

Care of tack

Tack is expensive and for that reason should be looked after but, even more important, clean, well-kept tack is more comfortable for the pony.

To clean tack, you need a bar or a tin of saddle soap, a couple of small sponges, a chamois leather and a tin of one or other of the proprietary saddle oils or greases, such as Kocholine.

New saddlery is always stiff and often bright yellow in colour. It needs oiling to make it soft and supple and also to tone the colour down. Nothing looks worse than a shining new bridle or saddle, unless it is a shining new bridle *and* saddle. It just does not look workmanlike, and I would never use either until I had spent a couple of evenings softening up the leather and darkening it.

The point to remember about leather is that it has two sides, an obvious observation, perhaps.

The outside is called the 'grain' side and in the tanning and dressing process has been given a virtually waterproof coating. The inside is the 'flesh' side which has not received the same treatment and is composed of thousands of pores through which the leather breathes and can receive nourishment in the way of oils and grease. Leather, in fact, is a living substance and its lifeblood is its grease content. In use it continually loses grease which has, therefore, to be replaced if the leather is to remain soft and supple. When leather loses its grease content entirely it becomes hard and brittle and can be snapped in the fingers.

To soften new tack take whatever preparation you have chosen and rub it with your fingers on to the 'flesh' side of the leather. In the case of a saddle, rub on the under side of the flaps and skirt, on the girth straps and on the panel beneath the flap. The grease will then penetrate into the body of the leather.

The 'grain' side should be treated with saddle soap applied with a slightly damp sponge and then finished off with the chamois or a rag.

Do not put too much grease on the outside of your saddle. It cannot penetrate and most of it will rub off on your clothes.

In a week or so, if you treat the tack regularly, it will have

Above: some of the items needed for cleaning tack.
Below: a saddle being put on quietly and correctly.

become softer and darker in colour.

After using tack it should be cleaned. Once it is soft it will need a rub over only, but at least once a week it should be cleaned thoroughly.

To clean the saddle remove the leathers, irons and girth. Clean off sweat deposits from the panel with saddle soap, and clean the girth straps and sweat flaps in the same way. Soap the top of the saddle and the flaps and finish off again with the chamois. Once a week apply grease in the way described.

Saddle soap your leathers and wash your irons in warm soapy water. If your girth is a leather one it will need greasing and soaping regularly as it will collect a lot of sweat deposit and will be losing a lot of its grease content because of its contact with the heated body of the pony. Nylon girths should be washed regularly otherwise they become hard and can cause chafing.

To clean your bridle you must take it to pieces and clean each part separately being sure to remove powdery, white sweat marks on the flesh side. If these are left they would block the pores and prevent grease from penetrating.

Wash the bit in the same way as the strirrup irons and once a week clean the bridle buckles with polish. If your bit and irons are made of nickel not stainless steel, they will also need polishing from time to time.

Keep your saddle on a saddle-rack, to prevent it becoming damaged. If you have to put it on the ground at any time, place it down gently on the pommel with the cantle resting against a wall. Hang your bridle, as in the diagram, from a bridle bracket.

Last, remember that leather has two great enemies, water and heat, as these reduce its fat content dramatically. *Do not* however dirty it is, soak your tack in a bucket of hot water. This practice will remove the grease and leave the leather dry and brittle. *Do not* for the same reason, dry tack over radiators or in front of a fire, just let it dry in a warm place.

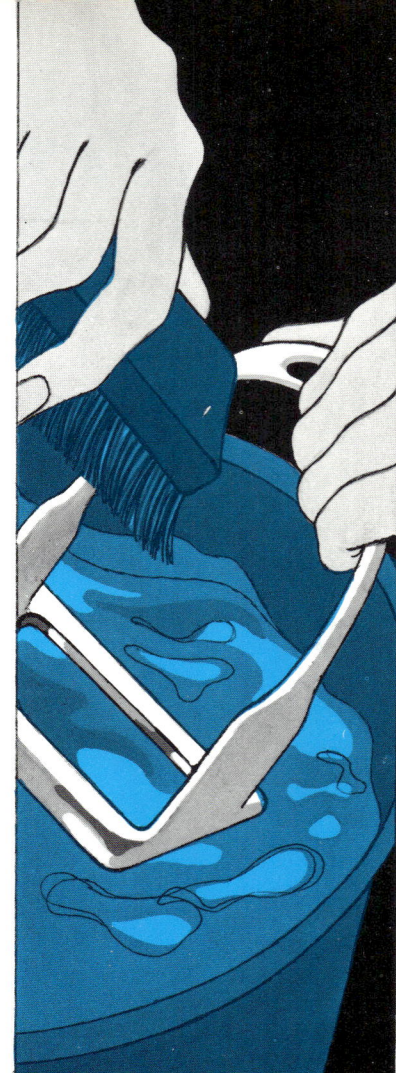

Above: cleaning stirrup irons.

Below: cleaning a saddle with saddle soap and sponge.

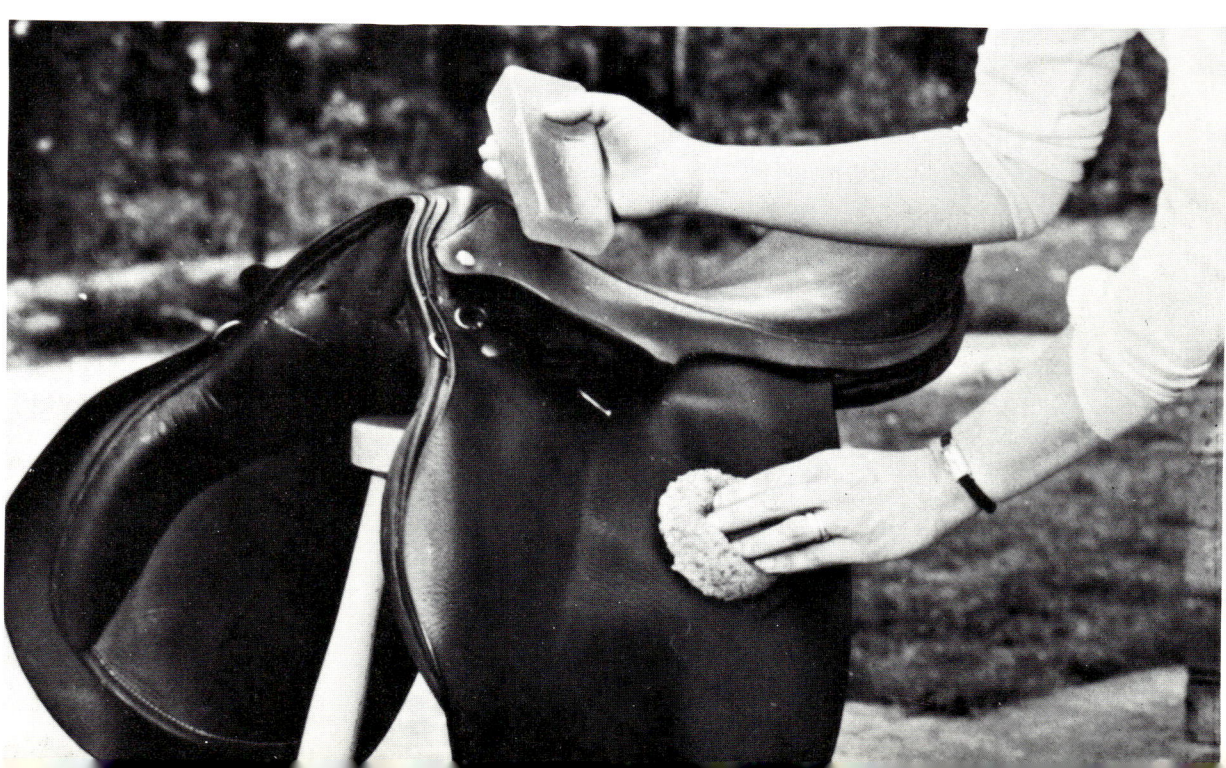

Pony Care

Most ponies spend the better part of their lives in a paddock, so when we are thinking about looking after a pony, our first consideration must be to provide him with a suitable field and then make the most of the area available.

An ideal paddock should (a) be *safe*, (b) provide such amenities as *shelter* and *water* and (c) provide a portion of the pony's *food*.

Above: a well-fenced paddock with a stable and water facilities. This is a 'safe' paddock which will supply quite a large portion of the pony's food.

Below: a drawing showing the construction of a post and rail fence.

Safety

To be safe the paddock must be adequately fenced so that the pony cannot get out on to roads and so on, nor injure himself on the actual fencing used.

Good, thick, natural hedges are one form of satisfactory fencing, but in their absence artificial fences will have to be erected. The best, and the most expensive, are those made from stout posts and rails well creosoted to preserve the wood and to discourage the pony from chewing it. A cheaper and almost as good a fence can, however, be made from *plain*, heavy-gauge wire strung tightly between solid posts set about 2·5 m apart. Four strands of wire are needed, and the lower one should not be less than 30 cms from the ground, so that there will be no chance of the pony catching his foot over the wire. Barbed wire is not suitable and is dangerous, as is chicken mesh.

Gates which give access to the paddock must be wide enough so that the pony can be led through easily, and they must be fitted with a good fastening arrangement that neither a pony nor careless people can undo.

Foreign bodies

All paddocks need to be absolutely free of any articles that might cause injury to the pony. These include pieces of glass, tins, oddments of metal and any of those horrid pieces of plastic with which careless folk litter the countryside. Plastic, if eaten by the pony, will do him no good at all and could cause very serious trouble.

Poisonous plants

Plants, trees and shrubs which are poisonous to livestock grow fairly readily in hedgerows and even on open ground. Many of them, if eaten in any quantity, are sufficiently toxic to cause death, and so paddocks on which ponies graze, and particularly the hedges, should be examined carefully and any offending growth removed.

    The most common of the poisonous plants are the yellow-flowered ragwort, briony, deadly nightshade, foxglove and hemlock. Privet, laurel, rhododendron and laburnum are also poisonous and, of course, yew, which is probably the most dangerous of all. Study the drawings of these plants and shrubs carefully and make sure there are none in your paddock.

Yew   Laburnum   Rhododendron   Deadly Nightshade   Laurel   Foxglove

Below: ponies prefer to live outside and are healthier when kept in this way, but they do need some form of shelter. This can be provided by hedges or trees, but where they are not available a three-sided shelter, such as the one pictured, is a necessity.

Above: the wild plants and shrubs of the hedgerow are pretty to look at but some can be poisonous to horses and ponies. Paddocks should be examined carefully and any offending plants rooted out and burnt.

Shelter

In very cold or wet weather ponies need some form of shelter. They need shelter, also, in the summer to get away from the worrying flies. A good hedge or a clump of trees provides a natural shelter but otherwise a three-sided hut, sited out of the prevailing wind, must be erected.

Water

The best way to provide a constant supply of water is to have it piped to a field trough. But the trough needs to be carefully sited, not placed, for instance, under trees, so that in the Autumn it becomes filled with leaves. Nor can it have sharp edges. It will, of course, need cleaning out at regular intervals and any scum that has formed on the water removed. Failing a water supply of this sort, arrangements will have to be made to carry water from the nearest point to a suitable trough. A constant water supply is one of the most important aspects of pony management. Ponies, and humans, can do without food for fairly long periods but not without water.

Stagnant ponds do *not* constitute a proper water supply.

A paddock, apart from being a place in which to keep a pony, can also supply a certain part of the pony's food requirements. How much it will supply depends on its size and on the quality and quantity of the grass it grows. A pony should live pretty well on about $1\frac{1}{2}$ hectares, although even then some extra feeding will be necessary, particularly in the winter when the nutrient level of the grass is at a minimum. Many ponies, however, do not enjoy paddocks as large as this, and the smaller the area the greater will be the need to feed extra artificial foods such as hay, bran, and nuts (a composite food containing all the necessary ingredients — nothing to do with the nuts from Brazil).

None the less, even the smallest paddock, if it is properly managed, will provide a quantity of feed. Rotational grazing is at the basis of grass management. This means resting one piece of land while the remainder is being grazed. Even a small paddock can be divided into two sections, and larger paddocks can be split into corresponding $\frac{1}{4}$ hectare strips.

The amount of grass provided by a small paddock depends, also, on the quality of the growth. Most paddocks, particularly if they have been hard-grazed by ponies for a long period, are of poor quality but an improvement can be made by having a soil analysis taken, and top fertilising in spring and autumn according to the soil's specific needs.

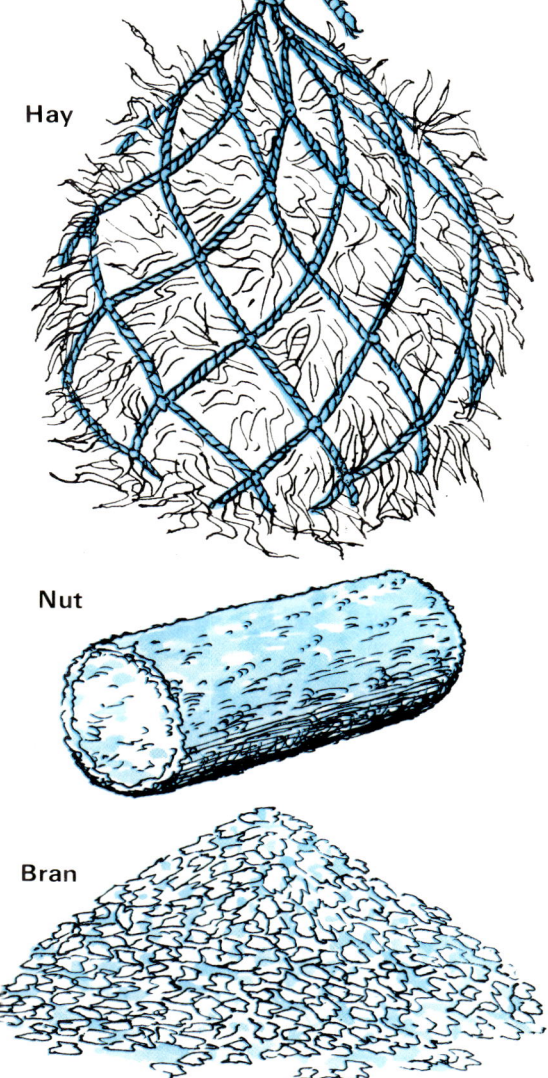

Hay

Nut

Bran

Above: many ponies will need the artificial foods shown here to supplement their diet.

Below: Wild ponies have to forage for their grazing.

Fertilising apart, the most essential point to remember about grassland grazed by ponies is the need to remove droppings regularly. If droppings are left on the paddock they will encourage a rank, lush-looking growth which the animals will not eat, and the available grazing area will be reduced in consequence. There is, also, another very good reason for removing droppings. The biggest danger to ponies living on small areas is that of *worms*, which are passed out in droppings and then enter the pony's system again as he eats the grass. All horses and ponies, throughout their lives, carry worms, and it is not possible to eliminate them entirely. However, if the worm burden becomes very heavy the result will be lack of condition, pronounced debility, anaemia and, in severe cases, death may result. Picking up droppings, which will contain the worm larvae (either *ascarids*, large white roundworms, or the more dangerous *strongyles*, the red worm), is one way of fighting the worm menace, but it is not sufficient on its own. *Every pony needs to be wormed at least twice a year*, and if living on a smaller area, even more frequently. There are lots of worming preparations on the market which can be given in the pony's food, but it is better to consult a veterinary surgeon before administering anything and then to act on his advice.

Finally, however safe you think your paddock may be, accidents can happen. Ponies can graze themselves or get a small cut just as easily as ourselves and it could be the cause of *tetanus*, an illness which is usually fatal. It can be avoided by the pony being given a course of anti-tetanus injections which will immunise him against the disease for life.

Above: this pair seem happy enough grazing in a lush field but every horse and pony carries a worm-burden and the worms enter the system as grass is eaten.

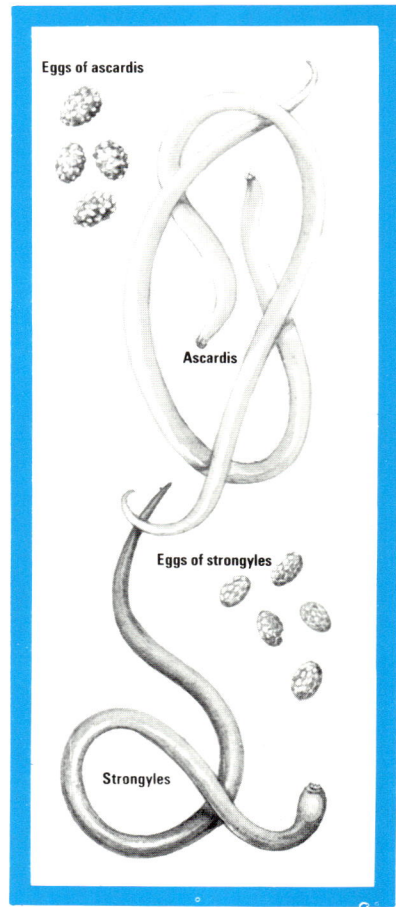

Eggs of ascardis

Ascardis

Eggs of strongyles

Strongyles

Right: a magnification of the large white roundworm and of the more dangerous red worm.

To catch a pony

Once your paddock is ready you will want to have it occupied by your pony. You will have no difficulty in putting the pony into the paddock, but you might find that persuading him to be caught to leave it is a different matter. The whole object of keeping a pony is to ride him, and if you have to spend a couple of hours a day catching him before you can put a saddle on his back, you are not going to ride him very often. So right from the start teach the pony to be caught. A new pony, who does not know you, and about whom you know very little, also, may decide that he will keep matters that way and when the grass is particularly good the temptation not to be caught up will be that much greater.

With a new pony, in the beginning, put him out wearing a headcollar to which you have attached a piece of rope about half a metre long. He must then be given an opportunity to get used to his surroundings, and to you, and is best not ridden for a couple of days. In that time, however, you can lay the foundations of trouble-free catching. Go to your paddock at least twice a day with a bowl of feed: nuts, carrots, apples and so on. Ponies, fortunately, are inherently greedy, even if they have plenty of grass to eat. Let the pony eat the food and as he does so you will find it quite easy to take hold, quietly, of the rope on his headcollar. When he has finished, make much of him and let him go. This way he will not always think of the food and your presence as a prelude to being ridden and made to work. At frequent intervals go and talk to the pony, taking an apple or a carrot in your pocket.

If you do this for even a couple of days the pony will learn to come towards you as soon as he sees you approaching. None the less, it is a wise precaution to keep the headcollar on for a week or two until you are quite sure he can be caught up easily.

Above: leading a pony in the proper, safe way.

Below: how *not* to set about catching a pony.

To catch your pony when he is not wearing a headcollar should present no difficulties if you carry out this simple training. There are, however, a few points to remember. First, do not go into the field carrying a saddle over one arm and swinging a bridle in the other hand. The pony knows exactly what use is made of those items of equipment and there is no point in forewarning him of your intention to go for a ride. He may not have the same idea. Instead, carry the halter or headcollar behind your back where he cannot see it, and if he does not come up to you straight away, walk briskly up to him, proffering the titbit and talking to him cheerfully. The best approach is one made from the front and at an angle — he may not see you if you creep up on him from behind, but when he does he will take fright. Get up close to him, standing a bit in front of his shoulder, give him his titbit and quietly pass the lead rope round his neck. Once that is in place you will have no trouble in slipping the headcollar on.

To lead the pony out of the field, or anywhere else for that matter, stand at his shoulder holding the lead a short distance away from the headcollar with your right hand and passing the spare length across your body to be held in the left hand. Now give the command, 'Walk on,' and walk boldly forward yourself. Nine times out of ten the pony will walk away alongside you. If he does not, then tap him with the end of the rope behind your back. Do not ever get in front of him and try to pull him along, he will only do the opposite and run backwards. Do not lead ponies, however well-behaved, with a finger crooked through the side of the headcollar. Even the quietest pony can become alarmed and shy sideways with the result that your finger gets pulled uncomfortably or even broken.

Above: carry the halter behind your back — there is no need to announce to the pony your intention of going for a ride.

Below: lead a pony this way and never with a finger crooked through the headcollar.

Outside in the summer

Most ponies, so long as there is enough grass and they are not asked to do more than hack about quietly, will be able to live during the summer without needing any extra feed. On the other hand, ponies that are regularly ridden, entered for gymkhanas, jumped and generally used pretty hard will not be able to do that amount and sort of work satisfactorily and still maintain good condition, unless they receive a proper ration of energy-giving food. Grass is all very well but it is a soft food that produces fat, not energy.

In fact, too much grass is just as bad as too little, and in some respects far worse. Ponies at grass spend the greater part of the 24 hours in a day stuffing themselves as hard as they can go. The result, when the grass is new and lush, is that within a week or two they look like little balloons on legs. In such an overweight condition the pony cannot be expected to gallop or jump, indeed, many can hardly trot with comfort. Extra strain, because of the excessive weight, is put upon the heart, the other organs, such as the lungs, and, of course, upon the legs and feet. By far the most serious thing that can happen, however, is for the pony to get an attack of *laminitis*. This is a form of acute inflammation within the foot itself and since the outer wall of the foot cannot expand, it causes excruciating pain and, of course, severe lameness.

This is another reason why it is a good thing to divide up your paddock, so that the pony's intake of rich grass can be restricted. If your pony still gets too fat, then you have to be cruel to be kind and confine him in a small area so as to keep him on very short rations.

Regular exercise, of course, will keep a pony's figure in order, but those working hard will need the extra food mentioned. The most convenient way to feed energy food is by giving pony nuts. Very few ponies need oats, which are heating and often make ponies silly and unmanageable.

How much extra food a pony will need depends entirely on the individual, his condition and the amount of work he does; some need very little, others quite a lot.

As a guide, however, a working pony will need not less than 1·5 kg nuts mixed with 0·5 kg bran and fed damp each day. Bigger ponies, over 13·2 h.h., will need correspondingly more and for a 14·2 h.h. pony between 2–3 kg of nuts would not be too much.

If the pony starts to lose condition, that is to get thin, then the ration must be increased. If he gets fat then reduce the grass intake fairly drastically.

Above: this is how a pony stands when suffering from laminitis. He rests on his hindlegs, trying to take the weight off the forelegs.

Below: this is how a paddock can be divided into strips. Not only does this method of strip-grazing conserve the available grass, but it is useful when a pony (because he is too fat) has to be confined in a small grazing area.

Outside in the winter

By September grass in a paddock has stopped growing, its feed value is negligible and it can be discounted as a source of food. In consequence, grass must be replaced by other foodstuffs. You must also realise that in cold weather a greater proportion of the pony's food is used in keeping up his body temperature. In severe winters, therefore, rations will need to be increased if he is not to lose condition.

The basic winter foodstuff is hay, which supplies bulk and also a certain amount of protein. The pony should be given as much hay as he will eat, which in the case of a small pony will certainly not be less than 4·5 kg a day. For the sake of economy it is better to feed hay from a net. If it is put out straight on to the ground, a lot of it can get trodden on and wasted. Tie the net up sufficiently high so that there is no danger of the pony pawing at it and catching his foot. It is a good plan to pass the loose end through the net about half way down and then to pull it tight and tie it again at the top so that the net is almost doubled. This will stop the net hanging too low when it is empty.

Ideally the pony will also need two 'short' feeds a day, which should be fed slightly damp, each consisting of 1·5 kg nuts, 0·5 kg bran and such titbits as carrots, sliced lengthways, so that they will not get caught in the gullet, apples, and so on. Larger ponies will need more but the only way to reach a proper figure is to study the pony's condition and how well, or otherwise, he is doing his work and to increase or decrease the ration accordingly. Once a week the pony will appreciate a bran mash which you can make in a bucket, adding boiling water to the bran and a handful of salt. The bucket should then be covered and the contents fed when they are sufficiently cool. Bran acts as a laxative when fed damp and in the opposite way when fed dry.

At all times, summer and winter, keep a salt lick in the field.

Obviously it is important to check that the pony is in good order every time you visit him and it is also essential to check the water supply. In winter make sure it is not frozen.

Grooming

Grooming not only keeps the pony smart but it is also very good for him. It keeps him clean and comfortable, it stimulates the circulation and, properly done, it builds and tones up muscle.

However, if a pony lives out all the year, the grooming he receives in summer must be very different from that practised in the winter.

In summer, the pony loses his coat, whilst in winter the coat grows thick and woolly to protect him against the cold and wet. Under the winter coat a layer of waterproofing, natural grease, forms and since this is part of the protective apparatus it must not be removed by brushing. So, if your

Above: picking up a hindleg, with the hand sliding down the inside front of the cannon bone.

Opposite: a selection of grooming tools.

Below: the right way to clean out a foot with the hoofpick, working from rear to front.

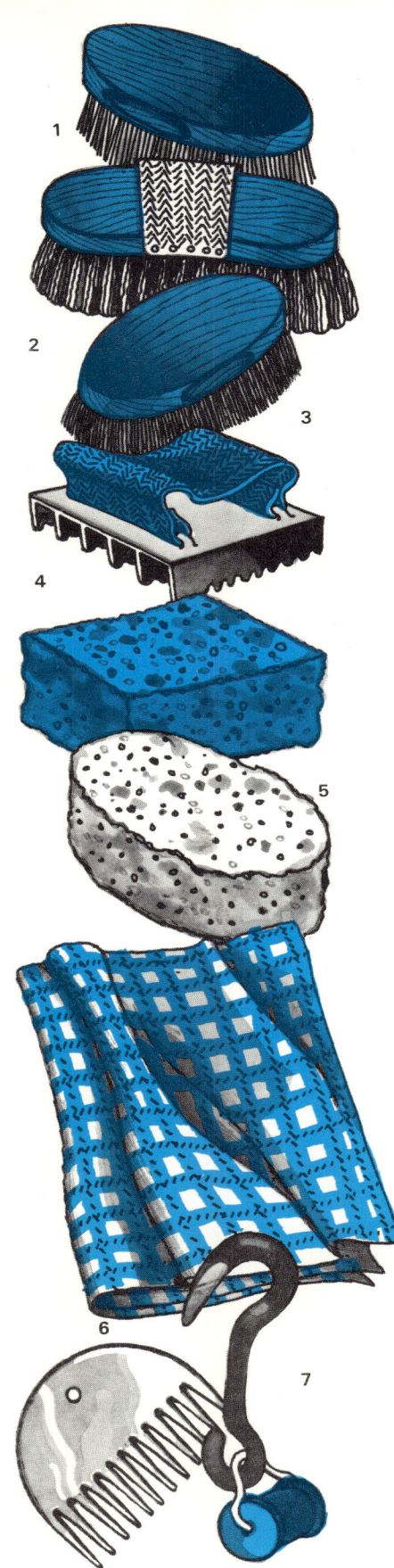

pony lives out in the winter, you will have to put up with his rather scruffy appearance and limit your grooming to removing the worst of the mud.

In summer, however, it is a different matter and you can groom your pony thoroughly. To do so you will need a set of grooming tools, which I suggest you keep in a linen bag which closes with a draw string These are the items you will need.

1. **Dandy brush** — a stiff-bristled brush for removing mud from the legs, and so on. It is too stiff and scratchy to be used on mane or tail.

2. **Body brush** — a soft brush used on the body and for brushing out mane and tai .

3. **Water brush** — a soft, boat-shaped brush used damp on mane and tail and to put a final shine on the coat.

4. **Curry comb** — a metal comb with a wooden handle used to clean the body brush — not the pony !

5. **Two sponges** — one for eyes and nose, the other for the dock.

6. **Stable rubber** — a linen cloth used to give a final polish.

7. **Mane comb** — a small metal comb used to trim mane and tail.

8. **Hoof pick** — a large one is best rather than a folding one.

Useful extras which could be included are an old brush for washing out feet, and a plastic curry comb which can be used on the body to assist the shedding of the winter coat. Finally, it is worth investing in a can of hoof oil.

When you groom the pony it is best to tie him up so that he remains in one place. Start by cleaning out the feet, using the hoofpick from the heel to the toe with the point facing away from you. If you have an old plastic bowl in which to catch the dirt so much the better. Pick up the legs this way: for the forelegs, stand at the shoulder facing the tail and pass your hand down the back of the leg, starting the movement by placing your hand on the shoulder, and letting it run downwards. Most ponies will pick up the foot at once but otherwise a push against the shoulder to throw the weight on the opposite leg, accompanied by a tug on the fetlock will usually do the trick.

To pick up a hind leg face the rear as before, run your hand downwards from the quarters to the hock and then down the inside front of the cannon bone. As the pony raises his foot, and they always do, slide your hand round the hoof and push it a little to the rear. Don't pull the leg too far backwards, to the front or to the side. Ponies do not like it and find it hard to keep their balance.

If hooves are very dirty they can be scrubbed out with an old brush. But do not overdo the washing as it removes the natural oils from the hoof. Be very careful, also, to see that the pony's heels are well dried after washing a foot. If they are left wet, the heels can become chapped and painful enough to make the pony lame.

To keep the feet in good condition and to make them look smart they can be regularly treated with hoof oil.

When the feet have been attended to you can begin the grooming proper. Take the body brush in your right hand and the curry comb in your left (or vice versa if you are left handed) and begin brushing high up on the neck behind the ears, working backwards from there so that the dirt and dust do not fall on to an area you have already brushed. Stand back a little so that you can put your full weight behind the brush and after every three or four strokes clean the brush out on your curry comb. Be very careful not to bang the bony projections on the pony's head with the wooden back of the brush, and do not thump the brush down over his loins where he is sensitive and where you could cause damage to the kidneys.

Brush the legs, particularly if they are muddy, with the stiffer dandy brush, but again be careful not to bang the knees or the hocks with the back of the brush. Now brush out the mane and tail, piece by piece, with the body brush. If you use a dandy instead you will only tear and break the hairs. When mane and tail are nicely brushed out, 'lay' them with a damp water brush. Clean out the eyes, nose and dock using both your sponges.

To put a final polish on the pony rub him over with a damp stable rubber.

Occasionally you may need to wash the mane and tail. When you do, use a good medicated horse shampoo which will remove any dirt, scurf and grease which may have accumulated. But do be careful to rinse all the soap out thoroughly.

Last, *keep your brushes clean*. Nobody ever cleaned a horse with a dirty brush.

Above: the easiest way to oil the pony's feet is to use a brush.

Below: to groom well you need to get your full weight behind the brush.

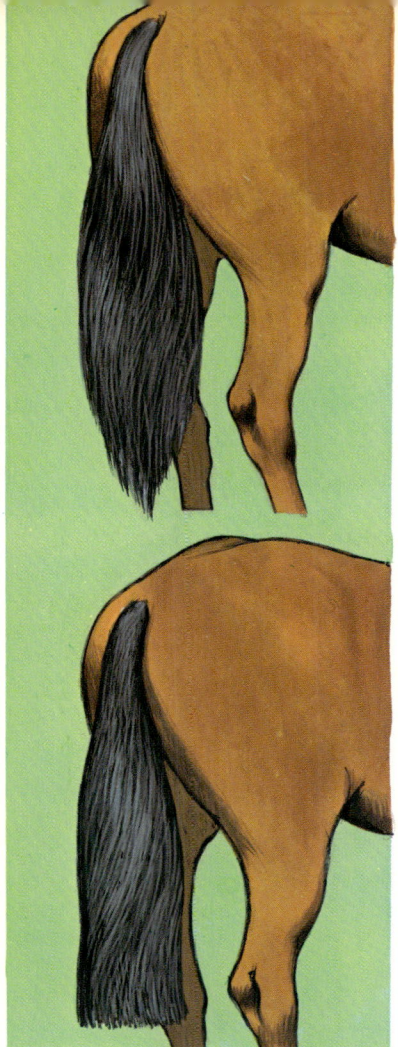

Trimming

To make your pony look really smart you will need to trim the surplus hair on his legs and to thin out his mane and tail. To accomplish the former you need a mane comb and a pair of sharp scissors. Comb the hair *upwards* and snip the ends off with your scissors. If you try to do it with scissors alone you will end up with a lot of unsightly ridges.

Never, on the other hand, use scissors to thin a mane or tail. You must pull the hairs out one by one *never* several at a time. Always pull the hairs out from underneath and not from the top. Have your tail absolutely clean before you start, then thin out the hairs at the top in the way described, either with your fingers and thumb or by using the comb, which you can push up to the root, twist and then pull. Allow about three weeks to get a really scruffy tail in order. If you pull too much at once you will make the tail sore and it is unlikely that the pony will let you do it again. If you want a really nicely shaped tail, damp it each day and put on a tail bandage for a couple of hours or so. Don't wet the bandage, which would then contract as it dried, nor put it on too tight or you will kill the hairs and make the pony very uncomfortable in the process.

You *can* pull the tail all the way down its length, narrowing it to a point at the bottom. It is then called a 'switch' tail. I prefer a tail pulled at the top and otherwise left fairly full with the end 'banged'. 'Banging' a tail means cutting it off so that it is square at the bottom. To do this, take a pair of long scissors and ask someone else to lift the tail up at the dock. Then calculate a hand's breadth below the pony's hock and cut the hair off in a straight line whilst making sure that you incline the scissors slightly upwards from rear to front. The tail when held naturally will then finish in a straight line. If you do not ask someone to hold the tail up before you cut then you will almost always finish up with a tail that is too short.

Above: a 'switch' tail, pulled to a point and a 'banged' tail, in which the end is cut off square.

Below: a pony being clipped.

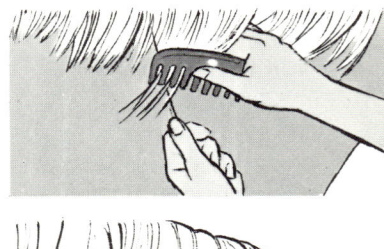

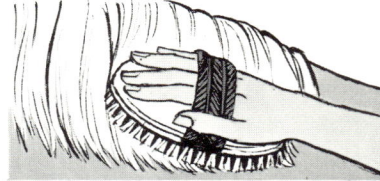

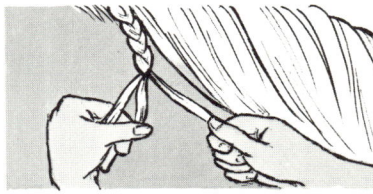

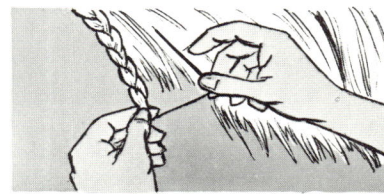

Manes

A really thick, unruly mane is difficult to keep clean and always looks untidy. To thin the mane the hairs are again pulled out from the underside. Brush the mane over to the opposite side to which it normally lies and then pull the hairs out with the help of the mane comb. You will then be pulling from the underneath side. You can take half a dozen hairs in the comb, pressed down to the roots, give a sharp twist and a pull and they will come out. Take a few days over the operation, however, and always pull from the roots. If you break the hairs they will grow again in upright spikes and will take months before they lie down properly.

The length of the mane should be about 12 cm, and anything more should be cut off with a sharp penknife rather than scissors, which can make a horrid, irregular line.

Plaiting

If you want to go showing or hunting you will probably want to plait your pony's mane and, perhaps, if he grows a very full tail, you will want to plait that too.

You can plait up a mane in two ways, either using a needle and thread and sewing the plaits in place, or by securing them with rubber bands of the same colour as the hair. The former, if done properly, looks the better of the two.

Before you can plait a mane it must, of course, have been pulled to a manageable length. There are all sorts of theories about how many plaits should be made, but the truth of the matter is that the number of plaits depends on the shape and length of the neck and what is pleasing to the owner.

The object is to improve the look of the pony and particularly of his neck. If the neck is long, therefore, it looks better with a lesser number of plaits than does a short neck. Weak necks are improved by plaiting loosely to give the impression of a higher, better line. Strong necks look better with small, tight plaits and so on. I use six plaits plus one on the forelock or, if the neck is a bit short, eight plus one.

First, damp and lay the mane then divide it into the number of sections required. Plait the hair and, if you are using a

Above & below: to plait a mane it must first be pulled fairly short over a period of a week or so. With the mane a manageable length it is then damped and divided into the number of sections required. If you follow the directions given in the text in conjunction with the diagrams you will find plaiting is quite easy – after some practice!

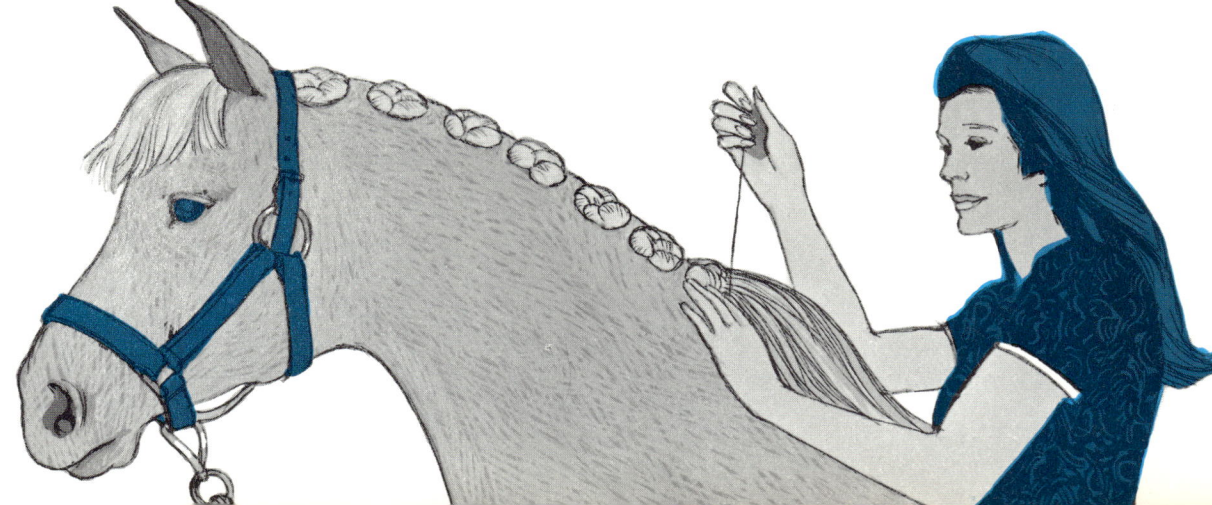

thread and needle, plait in a doubled over 25 cm length of thread about half-way down. When the plait is finished you have two loose ends of thread. Loop these ends round the plait and pull tight. Now thread both ends through the needle, double the plait under and bring the needle through as close to the base as possible. Pull the thread ends through, remove the needle and tie the plait firmly. Then cut off the spare thread ends.

It is much easier if you use rubber bands. You just loop the band round the bottom of the plait tightly, turn the plait under, and secure the whole thing with the same rubber band.

It requires a lot of practice to plait a tail well, but if you follow the diagram carefully you should, after a few attempts, make a fair job of it.

On the other hand, if you have a nicely pulled tail, well-shaped by bandaging, you do not need to plait it — in fact, it is impossible to do so because there is not enough hair. I prefer a pulled tail to a plaited one.

Shoes

In order to prevent the horn of the foot from breaking and to prevent the foot being damaged by hard going, ponies need to wear shoes and just as your shoes must fit so must those of the pony. That means that the shoe must fit the foot and not the other way about.

The foot is made up of a hard, outside wall encompassing a second, sensitive wall. The division between the two is made by the 'white line' which you can see if you look at the sole of a scrubbed unshod foot. The smith has to drive his nails into the hard wall and so there is very little room for a mistake.

Shoes, of course, wear out and, also, 'clenches', the turned nail ends, can rise up and can then cause injury if the pony catches the rough edges of his leg. Furthermore the horn, like our nails, grows about 0·5 cm each month.

For this reason shoes have to be removed every four weeks or so. If they are not worn out they can be put back on after the foot has been trimmed.

Above: from the top is a seated-out, fullered shoe; a plain shoe with a featheredge to prevent the brushing of one foot on the other; and a 'tip' shoe often fitted to prevent feet breaking when ponies are at grass.

Right: the way the hind leg should be held when shoeing.

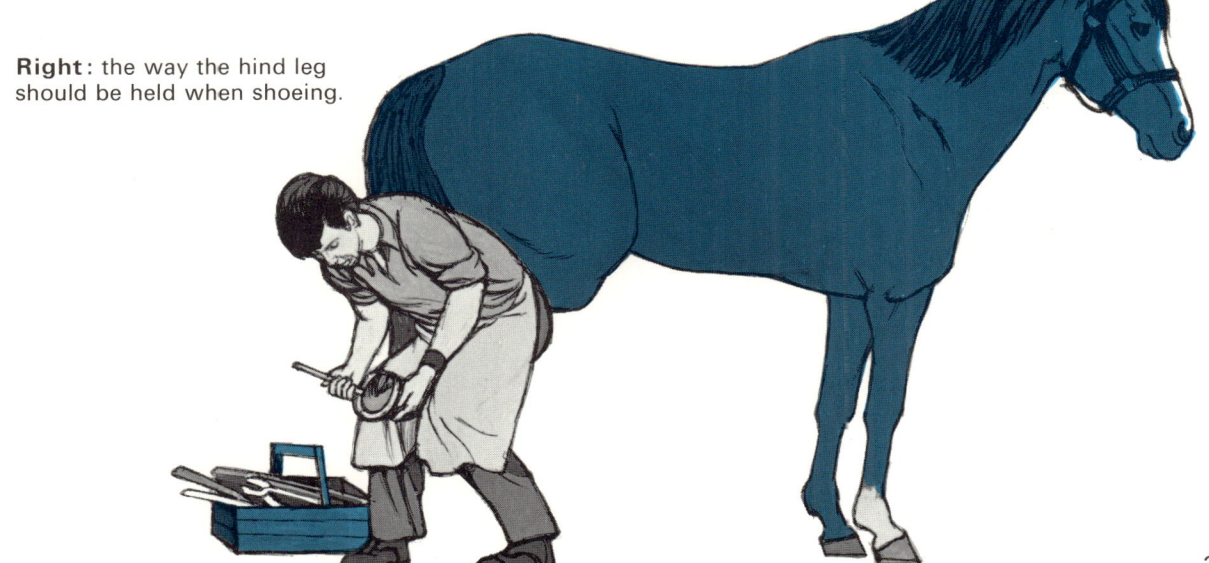

Failure to attend to the pony's feet regularly can spoil his action and even make him lame.

Teeth

Ponies and horses have six incisor or 'biting' teeth, and twelve molars or 'grinders' in each jaw. In addition, geldings grow 'tushes' behind the incisor teeth. Until the pony is about six years of age he does not have his full complement of permanent teeth. Up to that point he is still replacing his milk teeth. Young ponies, therefore, can feel discomfort when 'teething' just as humans do, but older ponies can also suffer tooth troubles.

Because the upper jaw is larger than the lower, with the molars growing down and outwards, whereas the molars of the lower jaw grow in opposite fashion, it is possible for wear to occur on the teeth leaving the enamel with sharp edges. Teeth in this condition can cause the inside of the cheeks to be lacerated, making biting difficult and uncomfortable and also preventing the pony from eating properly.

Once a year, therefore, and more if it is needed, ask the vet. to examine the teeth and file them smooth if they have got sharp or there is any other trouble.

Stabled ponies

Ponies are sometimes stabled in the winter for a variety of reasons. For convenience, in the case of a riding school, or because they are of Thoroughbred or Arab type and do not winter out well, or because they are going to jump or hunt regularly.

In the last instances, it is usual to 'clip' the pony. By clipping, which is done with an electric machine (a larger edition of that used in a barber's shop), the heavy winter coat is removed either entirely or in part. Some people, for instance, leave the hair on the legs as a protection against cold and thorns, and most will leave a 'saddle patch'. Quite often ponies are 'trace' clipped, as in the diagram. The reason for clipping off the coat is so that the pony will be able to work hard without losing condition by excessive sweating.

If the coat is removed in this way, however, it is necessary to provide the pony with rugs to keep him warm in the stable and to take the place of his natural coat. Usually clipped horses and ponies need an under-blanket and a shaped canvas night rug to go over the top. For travelling or special

Here are three types of clip.
Above: is the 'hunter' clip with the hair on the saddle patch and legs being left on.

Opposite above: is a 'trace' clip.

Opposite: is a 'blanket' clip.

Below: here are a number of types of rugs. From the left is a summer sheet of linen or cotton, a wool day rug, a jute or canvas night rug, and for outdoor use, a New Zealand rug.

occasions many owners substitute a wool 'day rug', often with their initials embroidered on it. After work, and certainly for travelling, wool leg bandages are put on over a layer of cotton wool to keep the legs warm and to protect them from damage when travelling in a box or trailer.

Stabled horses and ponies cause far more work for their owners, however, than those kept out in the field. A bed, usually of straw, but sometimes of peat or wood-shavings, has to be provided and this has to be cleaned out every day. Each day, also, the pony must be exercised for at least 1—2 hours, otherwise he will become too fresh and the inactivity will probably cause physical disorders, too, for example, digestive upsets, swelling of the legs.

He will need between three and four short feeds per day as well as a good ration of hay, which all takes time to prepare, and it will be necessary to groom him thoroughly at least once every 24 hours. Furthermore, the owner of a stabled pony must work to a strict routine. Ponies and horses are creatures of habit and expect their food at regular hours — if they do not get it they become excited, upset and confused.

People who cannot afford the time involved in keeping a pony stabled often employ what is known as the 'combined method'. This means that the pony is stabled at night, given a short feed and a good bag of hay, and after being fed and attended to in the morning is put out in his field wearing a New Zealand rug for most of the daylight hours. A New Zealand rug is a waterproof one, kept secure by an arrangement of leg straps so that it will keep in place when the pony rolls or gallops round his paddock. The advantage of this system is that the pony is able to exercise himself.

Common ailments

Fortunately, ponies are tough little creatures. If they are kept out they will rarely suffer from colds and coughs and they are not nearly so susceptible to illness as a stabled horse. None the less they can suffer from certain complaints and they are just as liable to cuts and grazes as anything else.

Wounds are, in fact, the most common of pony ailments. Simple cuts and grazes are treated easily enough by cleaning them with warm water, in which a handful of salt has been dissolved. Then the wound can be dusted twice a day with sulphanilamide powder or something similar. Tears or deep penetrating wounds are best dealt with by an expert and the vet. should be called at once in these cases.

Deep wounds and severe tears can cause either *venal* or *arterial* bleeding. If it is a vein that is causing the bleeding, the blood is dull red and the flow can be stopped quite easily by applying lots of cold water, using a hosepipe for preference.

Arterial bleeding, which occurs when an artery is punctured or severed, can be recognised by the violent spurts of bright red blood. It is, of course, much more dangerous. Until the vet. comes, the flow of blood can be controlled either by applying a simple tourniquet above the wound, towards the heart, or by fixing a tight bandage in the same position. Cold water should then be applied in the same way as described.

Colic is the horsy name for tummy-ache. It is caused by sudden changes of food, by poor quality or unsuitable foods, or, sometimes, if the pony has gorged himself unwisely on some especial delicacy. Ponies pastured in orchards, for instance, will often get colic through eating too many unripe apples.

Attacks of colic in ponies kept out are rarely severe and usually the pony just looks blown-up and uncomfortable. If, however, the pony starts sweating, kicking at his flanks and constantly getting up and lying down, the vet. should be called. He will give the pony a 'drench', a prepared colic drink, which will cause the bowels to work again and relieve the discomfort.

Laminitis has already been mentioned. The principal cause in ponies is overweight and lush grazing. Since prevention is better than cure, watch your pony's figure and act accordingly!

Itchy manes and tails are a frequent nuisance. They occur in the spring and summer and are caused by an overheating of the blood due to the rich grass. *Humour*, a pimply condition of the skin, also occurs for the same reason. This can be cleared up by feeding bran mashes to which have been added 100 g of Epsom salts or by giving a similar amount of salts in the drinking water each day for a week.

Bran mashes and salts will also prove to be a remedy for itchy manes and tails but it will also be necessary to restrict the grazing by keeping the pony in during the day. Sometimes, itchiness in the areas of the mane and tail are caused by parasites. They can be cleared by shampooing the parts with a medicated horse shampoo — never use a domestic detergent on a pony, it will cause an acute skin inflammation — and then by applying an anti-parasite powder.

Sweet itch is one of the most severe of the skin complaints and causes ponies great discomfort. The cause of sweet itch is not known exactly, but it is thought to be an allergy brought on by the combination of some constituent of the spring and summer grass and the rays of the sun. Whole areas of the mane, neck, withers and tail become irritated and inflamed and the pony tries to get relief by constant rubbing. As the condition progresses a yellow discharge is seen and patches of hair fall out. It is possible for the vet. to treat the condition with a course of injections but it is necessary to keep the pony in, out of the sun and away from the grass, and to cut out green foods. Benzyl Benzoate, applied every other day, brings relief and Kur-Mange applied according to the instructions is also helpful.

Lice: ponies in poor condition can suffer from infestations of these parasites, but they can also be picked up by quite healthy animals out at grass in the spring. The parasites are irritative and can cause loss of condition since they are blood-suckers. To get rid of them the hair must be clipped away and burnt and the pony treated with an anti-parasite powder.

Swollen legs: old ponies, those that are worked too fast on

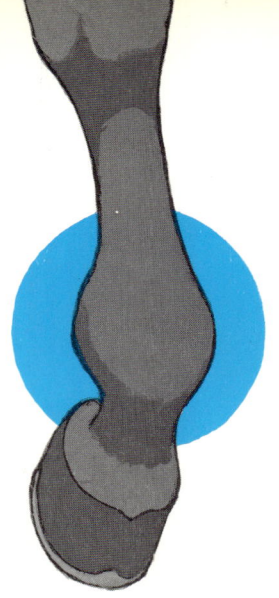

Above: swollen or 'puffy' legs occur round the fetlock joints and will feel hot to the touch. Puffy legs can be treated by hosing them daily.

Opposite: a dose of Epsom Salts is good for the blood.

Right: dirty or sodden conditions underfoot are a cause of thrush.

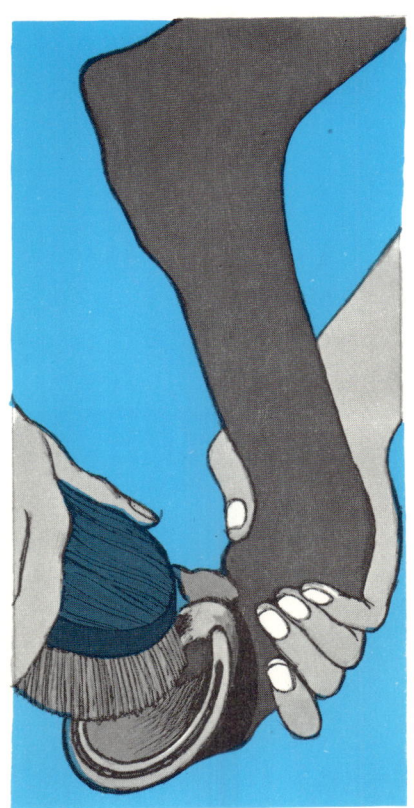

Above: dirty feet may be scrubbed with an old brush.

hard going, or ponies kept stabled without being exercised sufficiently may suffer from puffy legs in the area of the fetlock joints. A puffy leg will usually feel hot to the touch and may accompany a strain. Legs in this condition should be hose-piped for 10—15 minutes each day. You can also apply astringent linaments.

Mud fever is more serious. It is severe skin irritation, derived from muddy conditions, which affects the legs and sometimes the belly. It is more prevalent in some areas than others. The legs become very hot and swollen, cracks form in the skin and there is usually a thin discharge. The pony

will move stiffly and may, indeed, be lame. In severe cases the pony has to be stabled and heat treatment applied to the legs. However, the disease can be avoided if the pony's legs and heels are coated with an antiseptic ointment if ground conditions in his paddock are very wet and muddy. The ointment will also prevent cracked, or chapped, heels occurring.

Thrush is caused by dirty conditions underfoot and bad pony management. It occurs more usually in stabled animals but it can also occur in ponies kept out. Thrush can be identified by the foul smell of the feet, sweating of the frog and a discharge from the cleft of the frog. The feet need to be washed with disinfectant, the affected parts pared away and the foot dressed with Stockholm tar or copper sulphate.

Thrush, and all the trouble it causes, can be avoided by picking the feet out regularly.

If you visit your pony frequently you should be able to tell whether he is in good health or not. Healthy ponies look alert, have bright eyes and flat, shiny coats. In winter the coat does not have quite the same appearance but even then it should not look harsh and stary.

Signs of ill-health are a dull eye; a poor coat; a tight skin, instead of one that is loose and clean, and a general look of lethargy. The pony's droppings are also a good guide to his health. They should be well-formed, moist and not smell strongly. If they are hard, slimy and strongly smelling or if the pony has diahorrea there is something wrong and you should call the vet.

How to Ride

Saddling-up

Before we can ride the pony he has to be saddled and bridled and it is important to ensure that he is made entirely comfortable. If a girth is twisted or his bit fitted too high or low it will naturally make him irritable and distract him from 'listening' to our commands. Similarly, rough handling during the saddling process will upset him and in that frame of mind he is less likely to be co-operative.

Put the bridle on first, having made sure that the noseband and throatlatch are undone. Place the reins over the pony's head and then place your right hand at his poll. The bridle proper is held in the left hand and carried up the face until you can change the headpiece into your right hand. The left hand, very gently, passes the bit into the mouth over the tongue, without banging the teeth, and then both hands can be used to put the bridle over the pony's ears. When you have fastened the buckles check that the bridle fits, as described in Chapter 2.

Your saddle should have the irons run up and the girth, attached to the off-side straps, passed back over the seat. Put the saddle on well in front of the withers and slide it back into its proper place, so that the lie of the hair is not interrupted. Now fasten the girth. This is easier to do if you rest the flap on your head whilst you are adjusting the buckles. Most ponies blow out their bellies when being girthed but do not try to girth up too tight. Once the pony has walked a few yards he will stop holding his breath and you can put the girth up a hole. In any case, you will need to adjust your girth again once you are mounted. On the other hand, do not girth too loosely or your saddle will slip round as you mount and you and it will end up on the ground.

Run your hand under the girth to make sure it is lying flat and that no wrinkles of skin have got caught up in it. To make quite sure, you can take each foreleg and pull it out to the front.

Below & opposite: the four stages in mounting, but remember that when you have thrown your leg over, you must pause and lower yourself very gently into the saddle.

Above: illustrates the way to put on a bridle and then to check that nothing is too tight.

To mount

Stand on the near side at the shoulder, facing the tail. Take the reins in your left hand and rest it on the pommel. Have the reins just long enough for the bit to make contact with the mouth. If the pony is a bit fidgety have the near-side rein a little shorter than the other so that if he does move he will move round you and not away from you. With your right hand turn the iron, which should now be pulled down, outwards (i.e. clockwise), put your left foot in it, bounce off the back foot and straighten the left knee, whilst placing your right hand over the waist of the saddle. That is movement one, and is followed immediately by swinging the leg over the saddle, high enough to be well clear of the pony's rump. You then pause briefly before your seat touches the saddle, your weight being taken by your left hand on the pommel and your right hand, which has moved forward somewhere around the off-side skirt. Finally, and very gently indeed, you lower yourself into the saddle, place your foot in the iron and pick up your reins.

You will make your pony fidget and try to move off if:

1. You hold the reins too tightly.

2. You stick your toe in his ribs as you get up.

3. You kick his rump as you swing your leg over.

4. You land with a bump on his back instead of easing your weight on to the saddle.

You will find it easier to mount if you stand as close to the pony as you can.

Once aboard you can tighten your girth in the way shown in the diagram, without taking your foot from the iron.

Dismounting

To get off, take your reins in the left hand and take *both* feet out of the stirrups. This is much safer than leaving your left foot in the iron. That way you can be pulled over as you land if the pony moves, and you might even be dragged if he becomes frightened and takes off. With both feet clear of the irons the body is swung forward, with the right hand carried well forward on the saddle; at the same time your right leg is

brought over. Bend your knees as your feet touch the ground and you will land quite comfortably.

Do not get off by swinging your leg forward over the pony's neck. A lot of people do it, perhaps, but if you try this lazy way the day will come when the pony raises his head at the same time as you are swinging your leg. You will land up flat on your back, which serves you right, but you will also have frightened your pony.

Below: these are some of the exercises you can practise when mounted (so long as you have someone to hold the pony). They will improve your balance and make your body more supple.

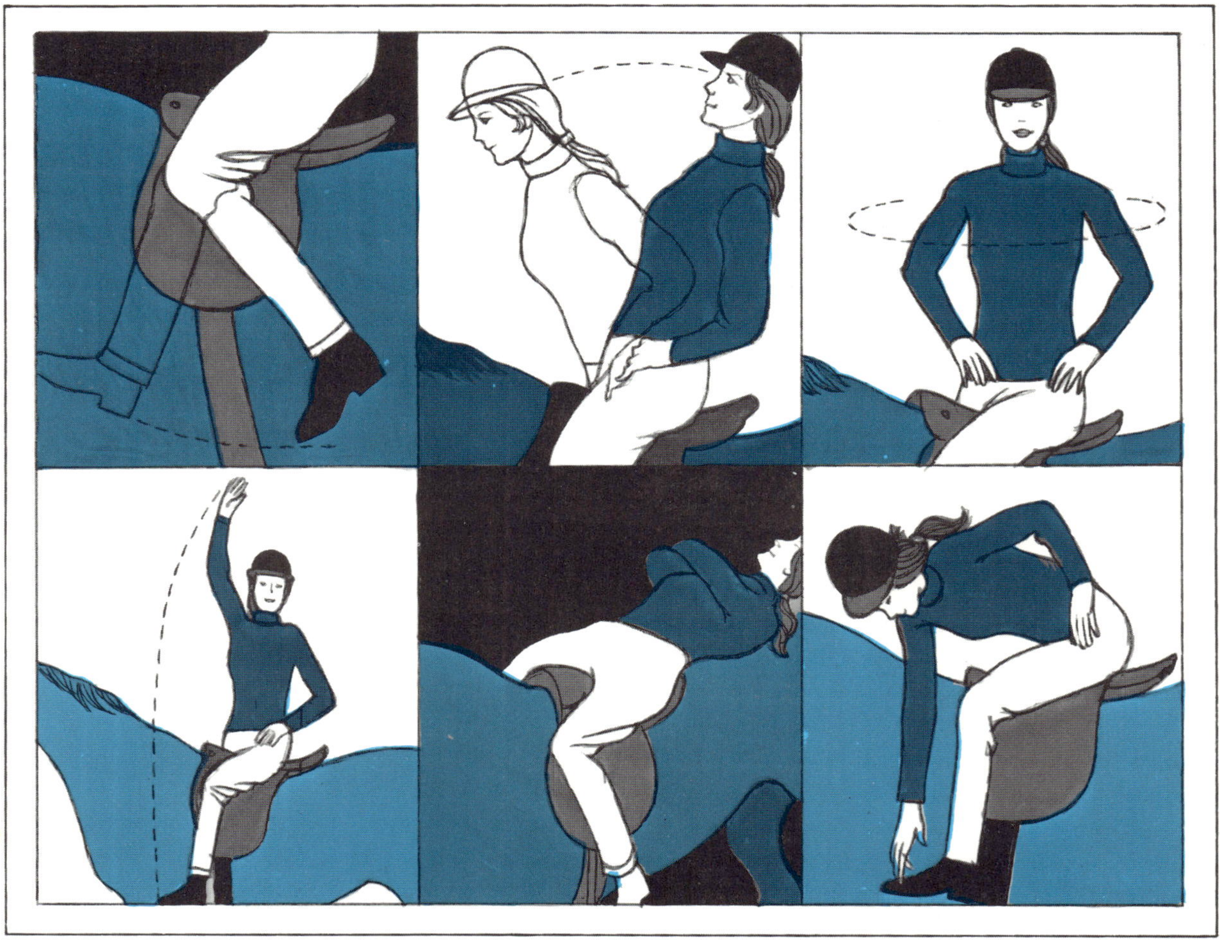

The seat

You can sit on a pony in all sorts of funny ways, sticking your feet out in front of you, gripping with your calves and so on, but if you want to be secure, in balance with your pony and in control there is only one way to sit — the right way. Until you can sit properly you will *never* be able to ride.

If you remember our discussion about the saddle and the need for it to position the rider over the centre of balance of the pony, then you will sit in the deepest part of your saddle, your back straight but not stiff, your leathers as long as you can comfortably manage and your lower leg drawn back so that it is lightly touching the pony's sides. In that position the legs are best able to give the 'aids' to the pony with the minimum of movement. Your toe should be raised and facing the front with the iron on the ball of the foot so that you do not lose that flexibility of your ankle. Do not push down with your heel otherwise you make your lower leg stiff. Hold your elbows lightly by your sides and keep your hands, thumbs on top, about 15 cm apart and just behind the pony's wither. The ideal is to have shoulder, hip and heel in one vertical line. Don't try to grip with your knees, this only prevents you from sitting deep in your saddle. Think of your pony as a barrel with your thighs and lower legs wrapped round it.

It is, in fact, quite easy to sit correctly whilst the pony remains still but it is rather more difficult when he starts to move. The best way to acquire a good firm seat is to have some lessons on the lunge. That is, you sit on the pony without your irons whilst the pony, connected by a lunge rein to the trainer, circles round at walk first and then later, when you feel secure, at trot and canter. Riding without irons gets you sitting deeper in the saddle and will make you ride with longer leathers when you come back to using your irons again. Since, on the lunge, you do not have to bother about controlling the pony, you can concentrate on sitting properly, with the instructor correcting your position.

Later on, still under the supervision of your instructor, you can do exercises, like those illustrated, which will help to

Opposite & above: these four pictures show the stages in dismounting. Points to watch are that you have both feet out of the stirrups at the start and that you make sure to swing your leg well clear of the pony's quarters in the second movement.

Below: this shows a nice length of leather which is neither too long nor too short. If the foot was taken out of the iron and allowed to hang loosely the iron would be on a level with the ankle bone.

make your body supple and improve your balance. Riding is, indeed, more concerned with balance than anything else, 'grip' and strength have nothing to do with it. In fact, if you try to grip with your knees your seat will be pushed upwards and it will be impossible to acquire a deep seat.

Once you have become confident on your pony and are able to sit without hanging on to your reins to keep your balance, you can learn how to control your pony by means of the aids.

The aids

Aids are the language of riding. They are the signals given by the rider to the pony asking him to do one thing or another. Obviously it is very necessary for the rider to understand the aids, but equally, if there is to be any satisfactory result, the pony has to learn the meaning of this set of signals as well. *You* may know that a squeeze with the legs means 'go forward', but the pony does not, anyway not until he has been taught. But we will deal with that in a following chapter, 'Schooling Your Pony'.

Aids are divided into two kinds, those that we call 'natural' and those known as 'artificial'.

The *natural* aids are those applied with the *legs*, the *hands*, the *seat and body weight* and the *voice*. *Artificial* aids, whip and spurs, act to supplement the natural ones.

The legs cause the pony to move forward, which he does by *pushing* with his hind legs. Our legs, in fact, control the horse's hind legs and also the position of his quarters. By

Below: the natural aids are those given by the legs, applied here behind the girth; the hands, shown here following the movement of the head, and the seat and the weight. The seat here is deep in the saddle and the arrow shows the supple back that keeps the seat well down.

46

applying them in certain ways we cause the horse to walk, trot and canter, we help him to turn *and*, yes, we can use them to slow down and halt!

Having created this forward movement with our legs the purpose of our hands is to control that movement. They regulate the speed and they help us, with the legs, to make changes of direction.

Our seat can, also, be used to encourage forward movement and the way in which we use our body weight will also affect the movement of the pony.

The walk

Before we apply the aids to make the pony walk, indeed before we ask for any change of pace or direction, we have to warn the pony that a request is about to be made. In fact, we *prepare* the pony. We do this by attracting his attention with a light squeeze of our legs and a momentary closing of our fingers on the reins. The pony is then attentive and waiting for the next order. To get the pony to walk from the 'prepared' position all that is necessary is to squeeze with the legs, which is like pressing the accelerator of a car, and to open our fingers to allow the movement forward, which is like releasing the hand brake.

Once the pony is walking we take up a light contact with his mouth, through the reins, and, since the pony has to move his head when walking, we must follow the movements with our hands. To reward the pony for obeying our legs we then cease to squeeze with them. We call this 'yielding' and it is something that follows every 'action' of the aids, whether the 'action' is made with either hands or legs.

If we want the pony to walk faster, we can 'act' with our legs by applying them alternately, in little nudges, in time with the movement.

Above: the spurs and whip are artificial aids used only occasionally to strengthen the natural ones.

Left: here is quite a good seat at walk, but it would be better if the rider was deeper in the saddle and had drawn the lower leg a little farther to the rear.

Position at walk

It is fairly easy to keep your position at walk but you must not let your body become stiff — it must follow the movement just as your hands do. Keep the head up and the shoulders straight, but keep the small of your back supple. In fact, follow the movement from the small of the back. The motion is rather like that used when you sit on a swing.

Halt

To come to halt from walk we prepare the pony as before, then: **1.** we *act* with both *legs*, which pushes the horse forward on to our *hands*; **2.** a bare second later we *act* with our hands, by closing our fingers; **3**. we *yield* with our legs, leaving them in light contact; **4.** as the pony slows down and halts in obedience to our request, we *yield* with our fingers. Then we relax and the pony will do the same. There is, however, a further aid we use to bring the pony to halt or to slow him down from one pace to another, and that is our body. At the same time as we apply our legs we stretch up and bring our shoulders back, behind the line they make with the hips. The effect is to put more weight on the pony's quarters and it assists the slowing down very materially. The same aids, omitting the actual halt, are used to slow down from one pace to another.

The trot

To make the pony trot give the preparing aids. Then: **1.** shorten your reins a little; **2.** act with both legs behind the girth; **3.** open the fingers almost simultaneously and incline the shoulders slightly forward. When the pony is trotting adjust the speed with your reins if necessary. If the pony does not trot freely on, continue to act with both legs, squeezing and yielding alternately. Never give a dead squeeze with either leg or hand, always apply and release, apply and release, which is the same thing as saying 'act' and 'yield'.

Below: at rising trot the rider comes out of the saddle and returns to it on alternative beats of the pony's legs moving diagonally in pairs. In these two pictures the rider is committing common faults. She is rising too high and when she returns to the saddle, her lower leg has slipped forward. In both cases she is behind the movement of the pony.

Position at trot

The head remains up and the shoulders open and straight but the body is inclined forward slightly. If you keep your legs in position you will find it quite easy to rise at the trot, i.e. sitting in the saddle as one diagonal pair of legs comes to the ground and rising to avoid the bump as the opposite pair touches down. With your body inclined a little forward your seat bones rise just an inch or two out of the saddle at one stride and then sink gently back at the next. It is only your seatbones which need to leave the saddle, your fork remains in contact. You will find it easier to start with if you count aloud 'one, two' rising at one and sitting at two in time with the two beats of the trot.

The sitting trot is more difficult to do well. If the pace is slow, which it should be, it is the suppleness in the small of your back which absorbs the bump. Your seat remains in the saddle and you must stretch down with your knees.

Above: here is a much better position at canter. The rider is sitting deep in her saddle and is going with her pony.

The canter

Aids are given for the canter to make the pony 'lead' with either his near or off foreleg. If you want to canter on a circle to the left then the left foreleg must lead, otherwise the pony will become unbalanced and is in danger of falling over. It is in any case most uncomfortable for the rider.

To understand the canter leads you have to appreciate that the pace is one of three beats, the trot, on the other hand, having two beats, and the walk four. In the strike-off into canter on a left circle, for instance, the first beat is made by the right hind leg, the second by the right diagonal, i.e. right foreleg and left hind leg together and the third beat is that of the leading leg, the left or near-side fore.

The easiest way to get a strike-off on the correct leg is to

49

apply the aids when the horse is entering a part of a circle. This is easy if you are going to canter in an enclosed school but even in the open the pony needs to be bent in the direction appropriate to whichever leg you want to lead. To canter left from trot the aids are as follows:

1. Prepare the pony and come into sitting trot for a few strides.

2. Bend the pony to the left, raise your left hand and close the fingers momentarily, keeping your right hand in contact but letting it go slightly forward.

3. Simultaneously apply your left leg on the girth, to keep the pony moving forward energetically, and act with your right leg *behind* the girth. This leg causes the corresponding leg of the pony to make the first beat in the canter sequence. For the canter right the aids, of course, are reversed.

Position at canter

The canter is not difficult. As you give the aid you must sit up straight, not lean forward which would put more weight on the pony's forehand and make it difficult for him to strike off. Thereafter your body should remain upright, swinging with the movement from the small of the back.

The gallop

The gallop is the fastest and most exhilarating pace but unless your pony is very fit he should not be made to gallop for other than very short stretches.

The gallop comes from the canter and is obtained by shortening the reins and using both legs actively. The body must now be inclined further forward so that your seat is just out of the saddle and your weight taken on your thighs and stirrup irons. At the gallop your pony will take a stronger hold of the bit, using it almost as a fifth leg to help his balance. You, however, must resist the temptation to take a continuous, dead hold. The hands must give and take with the movement, keeping contact with the bit all the time.

Below & opposite: these four pictures show the approach and the sequence of footfalls in the canter pace which is one of three-time.

Left: the turn to the right showing the left hand yielding as the right acts, whilst the right leg is applied on the girth and the left is held behind the girth, to prevent the quarters swinging outwards.

How to turn

Turning the pony calls for a combination of leg, hand and weight aids. To turn to the right, for instance, we *act* with our right rein by closing the fingers, and yield with the left rein by opening the fingers and carrying the hand a little forward, so that the pony is able to bend his head and neck, obeying the action of the right rein. Our right leg *acts* on the girth, whilst our left leg supports the right and prevents the quarters swinging over too far, by being held a hand's breadth behind the girth. The leg is then fulfilling the third function of the aids — it is 'resisting' to prevent an unwanted movement. Finally, you need to look the way you want to go. By doing so you are altering the disposition of your weight, placing it on the inside seat bone of the turn, and so encouraging the pony to make a corresponding change of direction. Do not, however, overdo the turn of the body; it is sufficient if the outside shoulder is slightly in front of the inside one, and keep your waist straight, do not let it collapse on the inside.

Unsaddling

At the end of your ride take off the bridle and saddle with just as much care as you put them on.

Run the irons up the leathers, before taking the saddle off and having done so put the saddle down carefully with its cantle resting against a wall. Slap the pony's back to restore the circulation before you take the bridle off. To remove the latter, unbuckle the throatlatch and noseband and bring the rein up to the headpiece, then slip the bridle over the ears with one hand whilst guiding the bit out of the mouth, making sure that you do not bang the pony's teeth. If you are turning your pony straight out into the field turn the pony so that his quarters point away from the gate before you take his bridle off, and leave yourself room to take a couple of strides backwards. Should the pony go off with a buck and a kick you will then be safely out of the way. Follow the same procedure if you are taking the pony to his field in a head-collar.

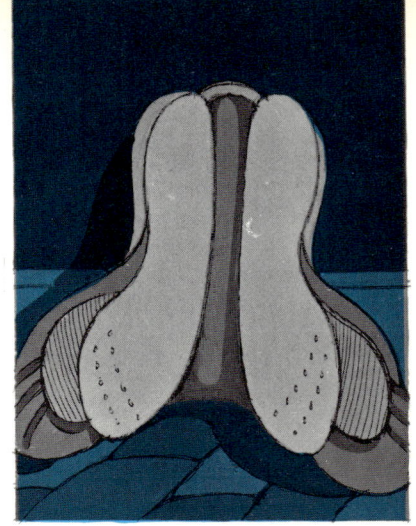

Below & above: when you have removed the saddle, put it down carefully with its cantle resting against a wall until you take it back to the tack room.

Hacking

One of the greatest pleasures to be had from owning a pony is the simple one of just going for a ride — 'hacking' we call it. But even this simple pastime has rules which have to be observed.

Ideally we want to hack over tracks and open country, but most of us are forced to ride on public roads, where there are all sorts of traffic, for at least part of the time. To do so in safety — your own safety, that of your pony and of other road-users — you must learn to obey certain simple rules, learn the technique of riding in traffic, keep alert and above all be good mannered and considerate, which really amounts to the same thing.

In Britain, where traffic is driven on the left side of the road, horses and ponies are ridden on that side and should keep well to the edge. As a matter of common sense and good manners, give signals with your arm if you are going to turn right or left or if you are going to pull out to pass a stationary vehicle, but only turn when you are sure that there is plenty of time for you to do so.

The most important thing to learn is anticipation. Ride, in fact, about 100 m in front of you and the same distance behind. In other words keep constantly on the alert for traffic coming either towards you or from behind. Your pony may be the very best in traffic but there is always the chance that he could be frightened by something moving fast, something that comes up upon him suddenly, or he may shy at a pram or even a piece of paper fluttering in the hedge. In any of those instances a nasty accident could result. Remember, his actions are not always predictable.

Above: when riding on roads give clear signals of what you are going to do in plenty of time, but check that the road is clear before you make the turn.

Below: If you are lucky, of course, like the two riders in this picture, you needn't ride on roads at all.

Above: bend your pony slightly towards oncoming traffic. If he shys he will then move towards the hedge and not into the road.

Below: remember your manners and say 'thank you'.

Traffic aids

When traffic is approaching you, particularly high, heavy lorries, slow down to a walk, a pace at which you will have greater control. The natural thing to do if you think your pony is likely to be nervous is to turn his head *away* from the approaching vehicle, but it is the WRONG thing to do. In the first place, the pony's vision is such that he will still be able to see the vehicle, but much more important is the fact that by bending his head into the hedge you are causing his hindquarters to move in the opposite direction, that is, out into the roadway. Should he become frightened in that position it is more than likely that he will swing his quarters, and the rest of him, into the road and into the path of the oncoming vehicle. So you do the opposite to what seems natural. Push your pony on with your legs, talking to him quietly and *without tightening* the reins, which could be a clear indication to him that you are as apprehensive as himself. Now, instead of turning his head away to the left, bend it slightly to the right and apply your right leg quite strongly behind the girth. If he should still take fright he will, because of his position, shy away into the hedge, which is far preferable to doing the opposite.

Apply the same aids for traffic coming from behind and the same again when passing a stationary vehicle.

Good manners

Most drivers will slow down for a pony and will pass carefully, but they are unlikely to feel quite so considerate if they continually meet riders who take up the whole roadway or who make no effort to acknowledge the courtesy extended to them. If a motorist slows down for you, thank him with a smile and a bow of your head. If you are a boy, touch your cap. It costs you nothing and it pleases the motorist, who is likely to continue driving carefully when he meets ponies. If there is a car behind you, unable to pass because the driver cannot see the road in front, wave him on with a smile when you are quite sure the road is clear.

Saddlery

Before riding on roads, or anywhere else, check that your saddlery is absolutely safe. Never ride bareback on roads or with only a headcollar instead of a bridle. And NEVER ride without a HARD HAT.

Wind and rain

On roadways ride extra carefully if it is a windy or rainy day. Ponies and horses are always a bit edgy in conditions of high wind, largely because they cannot hear so well and because the wind makes for greater and sudden movements of trees and hedges as well as blowing about leaves, twigs, bits of paper and so on. On wet days, motor-car tyres make a swishing noise and sometimes spray is thrown up by passing vehicles. Both can frighten a normally calm pony.

Bridleways

Almost every area has its proportion of open country, but it is not there for you to ride over unless it is common land. Because you are riding a pony do not think you have any right at all to ride over other people's property — you have not! There are, however, bridleways on which it is permissible to ride, but you must keep to the paths and not ride your pony in any fields that might adjoin them, however tempting it may be. You may not think you will do any harm by galloping over a field of grass, but to the farmer grass is just as much a crop as barley or wheat. Bridleways are usually of ancient origin but not many people realise how the word came into our vocabulary. It started when Henry VII decided to make a royal progress through his kingdom with his new bride, Elizabeth of York. The paths and roadways over which they travelled, often cleared in advance of the royal party, were termed 'Bridalways' and so the word came into our language.

There are, of course, other means of access to the country-side in the form of footpaths, but by law, in Britain anyway, these are reserved for walkers and ramblers and it is an offence to ride on them. If ponies and horses were to use these paths the going would soon get cut up and the routes made impassable.

Above: when riding in the countryside keep to the bridle paths and don't go into adjoining fields.

Below: a gallop is fun — but you don't have to wave your arms about, do you?

Trot, canter and gallop

On the roads it is better to walk. There is no harm in trotting *slowly* for short periods but you should not let your pony hammer away at a *fast* trot, which causes tremendous concussion to the feet and lower limbs and may result in all sorts of troubles. Remember that the concussion is accentuated by your weight on the pony's back. Many roads have grass verges and on these, so long as there is no bye-law prohibiting their use by riders, you can trot safely and, if they are wide enough, have a canter as well. Everybody who rides will have some favourite place for a canter or gallop, but such places should be used carefully. If you always canter or gallop in the same place it becomes a habit with the pony and you will find it very difficult to walk or trot even if you want to do so. So be sensible. Have your gallop by all means, but not every day in the same place. Resist, also, the temptation to go faster every time you meet a piece of grass. If you do not you will end up with a pony that *expects* to gallop every time his feet touch grass and that may not always be convenient or desirable.

Uphill and downhill

When riding uphill you can walk, trot or canter according to the steepness of the gradient and the type of going underfoot, but remember to get your weight forward so that the pony can make full use of his quarters. If you have difficulty in getting forward take hold of a piece of his mane.

Riding downhill is a little more difficult, particularly if the pony is not well-balanced. The result, in that case, is for him to go faster and faster until by the time he reaches the bottom he is galloping flat out to save himself from falling over. On gradual descents he will have no trouble but on steep ones it is best to go slowly. If you have to make a very steep descent approach it absolutely straight. If you try to go down sideways the pony can easily lose his footing and slip up.

At the end of the ride

A good rule is never to bring a pony home hot and sweating and to avoid this the pony should be walked for the last mile or so to give him a chance to cool off. Overheated ponies can easily catch colds and chills.

If you do bring a pony home warm, then give him a good rub down with either an old sack or a good handful of straw before turning him out to have a roll. If he is really hot you will have to walk him round for a good hour until he is cool, in addition to rubbing him down — and serve you right!

Above: uphill, get your weight forward so that the pony can use his quarters. Downhill, you can sit a little more upright, but if it is a steep descent keep your pony straight and go slowly.

Enjoying the countryside

You can increase the enjoyment of riding through the country-side by learning something about the crops that are grown in it, the variety of trees, plants and shrubs it contains, and the animal and bird life it contains. Surprisingly, you can often see more of the country's wild life from a pony than you can from your feet. You will certainly see squirrels, rabbits and hares and, if you get up early enough, you may have the thrill of seeing a fox returning to his earth after a night's marauding. In some parts of the country you may even be lucky enough to catch glimpses of deer. Look about you always and perhaps next time you go out for a ride you will see and recognise the trees, plants and crops.

Finally, observe the code of the countryside. If you have to pass through gates be sure to shut them after you, since they may be enclosing a herd of cows or a flock of sheep. **Don't** break down hedges. **Don't** ride on crops — keep to the paths. And **don't** be a litter-bug! If you take sandwiches with you or chocolate, keep the wrapping in your pocket to put in the dustbin when you get home. If you take, for example, a can of lemonade with you, take the empty container home — **don't** throw it in a hedge or in a field where it is unsightly and can be dangerous to both domestic and wild animals.

Below: observing the variety of trees, plants and animal life increases the enjoyment of a ride in the countryside, but do remember to observe the country code.

Schooling Your Pony

Perhaps it has never occurred to you that it is necessary to school, or teach, your pony. Perhaps you thought that riding was just a matter of jumping on, giving a kick when you wanted to go forward and a haul on the reins when you wanted to stop. Well, if you did, as you should now know, you were very wrong.

Just as children need to go to school to learn to read and write, so ponies have to be taught what is wanted of them and, in addition, have their muscles developed so that they are physically able to carry out our wishes. They are not born understanding the meaning of the 'aids'. It is the riders who have to teach them and they cannot do that until they themselves have learnt the language.

Just as important is the body development of the pony. He can gallop, make quick stops, and turn swiftly one way or the other easily enough when he is playing in his field, but it is quite a different thing when he has a weight on his back, which may be upsetting his balance continually.

The objects of schooling are to teach the pony the meaning of the aids and to be obedient to them, and second, but just as important, to make him physically capable of obeying the aids. An unschooled pony does not understand what we want and probably could not do what was asked of him even if he did. As a result he is not much fun to ride. A schooled pony, on the other hand, is a pleasure to ride, willing, obedient, and much more comfortable.

Left: the early training of the pony is carried out on the lunge when the pony describes a circle round the trainer. Lungeing strengthens, supples and balances the pony as well as teaching him obedience.

The early training of the pony, like that of the rider, takes place on the lunge. An enclosed area is needed for lungeing and a lunge rein, lunge cavesson and long whip. Finally, you need an assistant to lead the pony round you until he gets the idea of circling you. The purpose of the long whip is to encourage the pony to go forward and to remain out on the circle — it is never used to hit the pony. The reasons for lungeing are: **1.** to teach obedience to the voice — the pony will soon learn the meaning of 'whoa', 'walk on!', 'terrot!'; **2.** to improve the balance, and **3.** to develop his muscles and to make them equally supple on both sides of his body. Th s last point is very important. All ponies have a 'stiff' side. Usually this is the right side and it is not helped by our handling and leading them always from the near, or left, side. This bends the pony to the left but stretches and stiffens the muscles on the right side so that he has difficulty in bending his body in that direction. Much the same, of course, happens in people who are either right-handed or left-handed although in the human case it is usually the right hand that is favoured.

It is because of this 'stiff' side that most ponies will have more difficulty in turning to the right on circles and so on. Lungeing, if practised on both reins with greater emphasis being given to the 'stiff' side, will stretch and supple the b g muscles on either side of the body equally, since, if the lungeing is carried out correctly, the pony must bend his body from poll to tail to conform with the shape of the circle.

When the pony is ridden we can continue to ride him in circles or at any rate on elements of circles. To do so, a flat, enclosed area is needed, about 40 m × 20 m in size, although you can manage with less space. An arena, or school, like this can be made in a corner of a field where the natural fences will provide two of the sides. The other two can be marked out with small drums, painted white to look neat, or with large stones or stakes driven into the ground. If you think you might like to practise dressage tests, it is a simple matter to make hardboard markers and place them round the arena as shown in the diagram.

Below: if you want to practise dressage tests, make an arena on the lines of the one shown below.

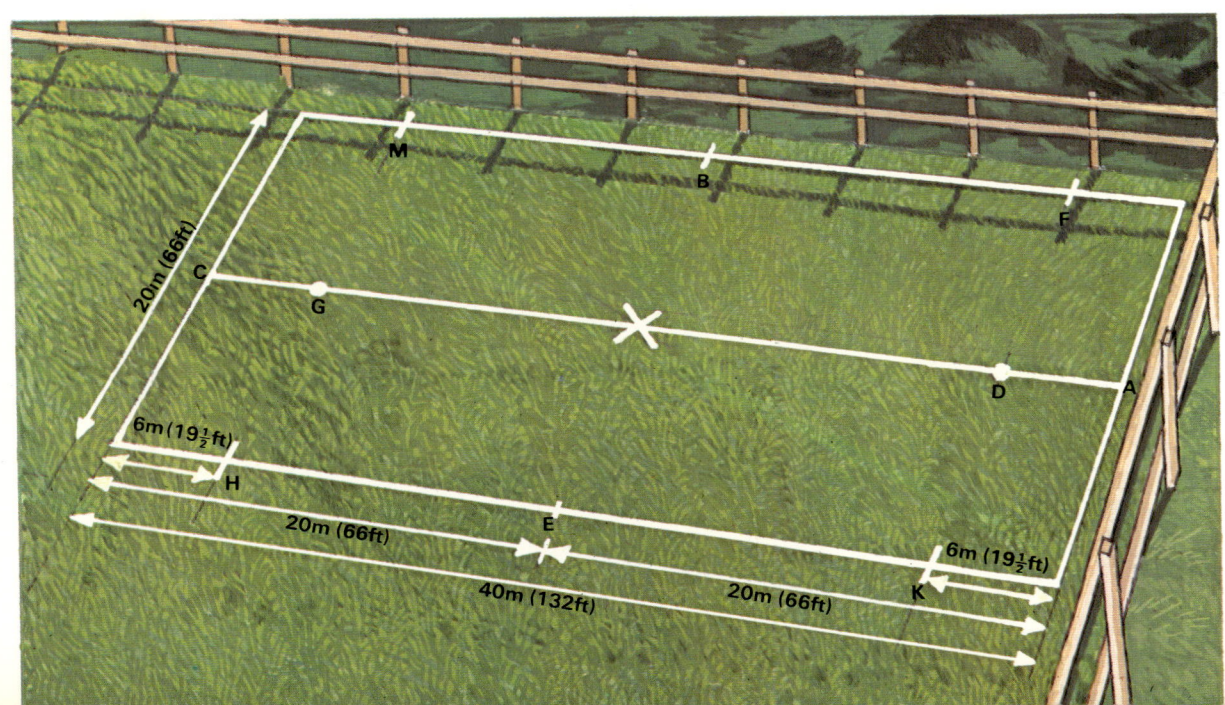

Even a schooling area as simple as this will give the pony the feeling of being enclosed and will help him to concentrate. It will, of course, help you to ride accurately too. The middle of a large field will not do. It offers too many distractions to the pony and he is unlikely to settle down and concentrate on his work.

To start with, you can ride round the school at walk, changing the rein by crossing the school diagonally, and taking care that you ride the pony deep into the corners and get him to bend round them correctly.

If your pony has received very little schooling you may find that he does not move off from halt very willingly, and that he does not, in general, respond to your legs. He should respond to the lightest of squeezes — it should not be necessary to kick, which loosens your seat and is, in any case, nothing to do with good riding. After all if it is necessary to kick hard to make the pony walk, what are you going to have to do when you want him to canter?

Below: try riding these schooling figures first at walk, then at trot. At trot you can rise on the big circles and sit on the small ones.

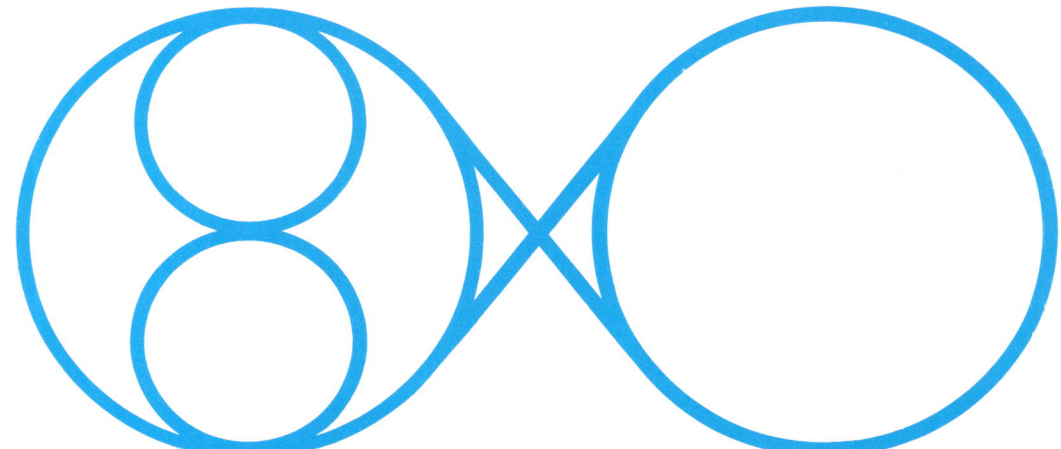

To teach the pony to answer your legs immediately ask someone to walk up behind him, encouraging him to move forward, the moment you touch him with your legs. He will learn quickly enough what is wanted, but the response can be sharpened if you carry a long whip and, without taking your hand off the rein, give him a quick tap behind your leg immediately you have given the aid to move forward.

When your pony moves away from the lightest touch of your leg and will come easily back to halt from walk with the help of the usual aids *and* your voice, you can begin to school at trot, working up to riding figures in the school, similar to those illustrated. If you ride the pony correctly, pushing him with your legs into your hands and keeping the pace fairly slow and rhythmical you will soon find that his way of going is improved, that he feels better balanced and that he has little difficulty in carrying out the various movements.

Once this stage is reached at trot, you can start working at canter, using the full arena to start with and then, when he can canter easily round, riding full circles on either rein using one or other end of the school. If the pony finds it difficult to strike off correctly into canter at the corners of the school, that is if he does not strike off on the correct leading leg, or even if he does not get into canter at all but just trots faster, you can help him by putting a pole across the corner of the school. You must first, however, get him used to the pole by walking and trotting him over it. Then you can raise it a little from the ground by resting it on a couple of bricks. If you approach the pole at a strong (not a runaway) trot, the pony will hop over it and in nine cases out of ten will fall straight into canter and on the correct leg, too.

The pony will be made more obedient, increasingly supple and acquire a better balance by being made to practise the 'transitions', that is the changes of pace from walk to trot to canter and vice versa. 'Upward transitions' are those from a slower pace to a faster one and 'downward' transitions are those made from faster paces to slower ones.

The balance, and the obedience and suppleness of the pony, is also improved by varying the speed of each pace. Highly-schooled horses and ponies can move at three 'speeds' within each pace, i.e. ordinary, collected and extended. Unless the trainer is skilful, however, these three forms of any one pace are difficult to achieve correctly and it takes time.

None the less, it is quite possible to teach a pony to shorten and lengthen his stride, although both may be very far from 'collection' and 'extension'. In 'collection' a highly-trained horse carries his neck and head high, the latter in an almost vertical position. He moves with a shorter, higher stride, his croup is lowered significantly and his hindquarters are engaged well under his body. In fact the whole outline of the horse is shortened. In extension it is lengthened and the stride increased accordingly.

At walk the pony can be made to shorten his stride by the rider acting with the legs and at the same time resisting, intermittently, with the fingers of the hands. As a result the pony is compressed between the legs at one end and the hands at the other, and so the quarters are engaged more actively, the head is raised and the stride shortens. To extend at walk, the legs act, but tactfully, otherwise the pony trots, whilst the hands continue to follow the movement of the head without resisting.

Much the same happens at trot but then it is easier if the rider 'sits' instead of rising when the shortened trot is asked for. A good exercise at trot is to ride round the arena rising, going into sitting trot between the corners at the 'short' sides, or even making a full circle at sitting trot at each end of the school. This can be followed by pushing the pony into an 'extended' trot across the school diagonally when the 'short' side has been completed at the shortened, sitting trot. It is as well to rise to the trot when extending the pace.

At canter the easiest way to shorten the stride is to act with the inside rein to bend the pony's head towards his leading foreleg, i.e. left on the canter left and vice versa. The effect is to restrict the movement of the inside shoulder and consequently shorten the length of stride taken. To extend the

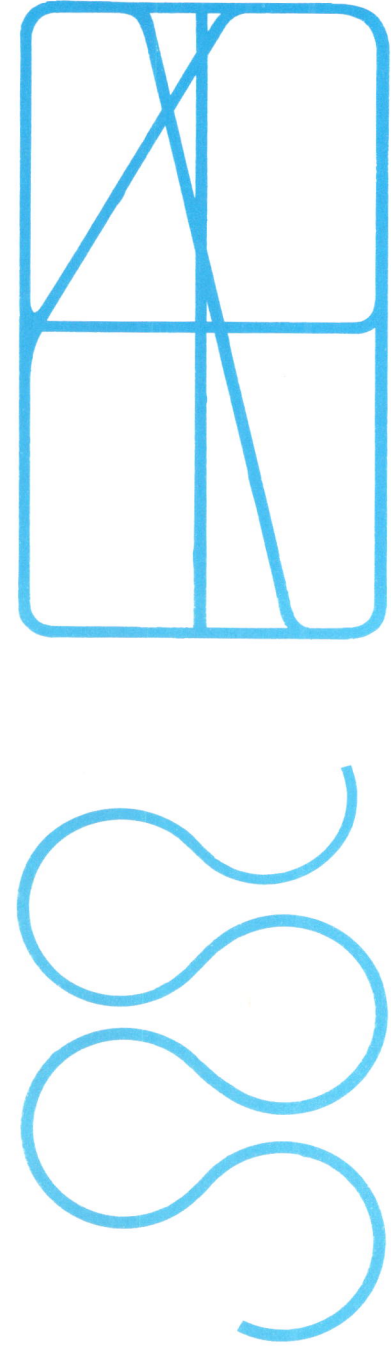

Above: the top figure shows a variety of ways in which you can change direction within the arena. The bottom figure shows a serpentine using the whole area. This is an excellent suppling exercise for a pony, but until he is well-schooled you will find it is not easy to do smoothly and accurately.

stride the inside shoulder is freed by using the opposite, outside, rein to bend the head slightly towards the wall of the arena. Practise first the extended canter down one long side, counting aloud the number of strides taken, then shorten the canter and see how many extra strides are involved.

From this point more use can be made of poles on the ground as a strengthening exercise and also as an introduction to jumping. Place a pole on each of the long sides and walk and trot over them. A hop or a little jump over the pole is not wanted, the pony should pass over the poles without hesitation and in absolute calm. We can then add two or even three more poles to each side, placing them on the ground to form a grid, each pole being about 1·5—2 m apart. It is difficult to give an exact distance since this depends upon the size of the pony and his length of stride. A small pony with a short stride will probably find 1·25 m a comfortable distance but the exact spacing can only be determined by trial and error.

Below: crossing a grid of poles at walk. This is the first exercise in jumping. To be critical, the leading rider has her elbows too straight and in consequence her hands are fixed and not following the pony's head.

Crossing the grid at trot causes the pony to stretch out his head and neck, to see where he is going, and makes him use his hindquarters more actively. The result is a rounding of the back with the hindlegs being brought well under the body. To carry out the exercise the rider must rise to the trot and whilst driving forward with the legs must be prepared to yield with the hands to allow the extension and lowering of the head and neck. The next stage involves raising the poles from the ground, which will cause the pony to raise his legs higher and to make even more use of his body.

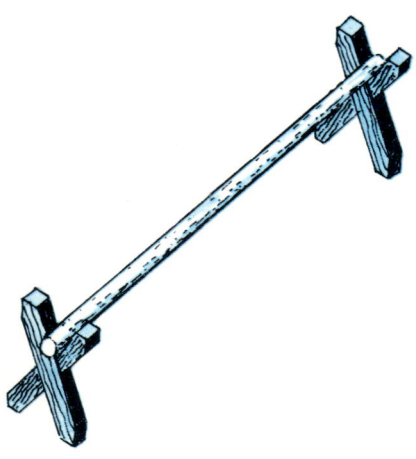

The poles are quite suitable for this purpose but to prevent them being knocked down they need to rest on thick chunks of log in which a vee has been cut. The ideal is to use cavalletti, very versatile pieces of equipment which are not difficult to have made.

A cavalletto (the singular form of the Italian word meaning 'little horse') is a stout pole supported by two cross-pieces. By turning the cavalletto three heights can be obtained, usually about 25 cm, 35 cm and 50 cm.

The cavalletti can be placed in the same way as the ground poles, and at their lowest height, and trotted over as before.

So far the cavalletti have been used as a balancing and strengthening exercise but they can now be employed to teach the pony to jump. Initially all that is required is to move the third cavalletto of a grid of four up to the last one. The pony then trots over the first two and jumps over the final pair. The last two can then be placed one on top of the other, sloping away from the approach to make something looking like a real fence, even if it is less than 60 cm high.

Most ponies will soon jump quite freely if they are introduced to jumping fences gradually in this way, and are never overfaced by the rider asking them to jump something which is too big for them, or asking them to jump too frequently. Nothing stops a pony jumping freely so quickly as too much jumping. It only makes him bored, sour and resentful. Similarly, ponies will stop jumping if, because of their riders' incompetence, it becomes an unpleasant experience. If, for instance, a pony receives a jab in the mouth every time he jumps a fence (because his rider has lost her balance and has to stay in the saddle by hanging on to the reins) he will very quickly decide that there is no future in leaving the ground — and act accordingly. Who can blame him?

If you are not very experienced at jumping, the ideal is to take some lessons on a good jumping pony, with an instructor, before you try to teach your own pony to jump. On the other hand, if this is not possible, then there is even more reason for you to follow the schooling system described so that you get the feel of a jump by easy stages.

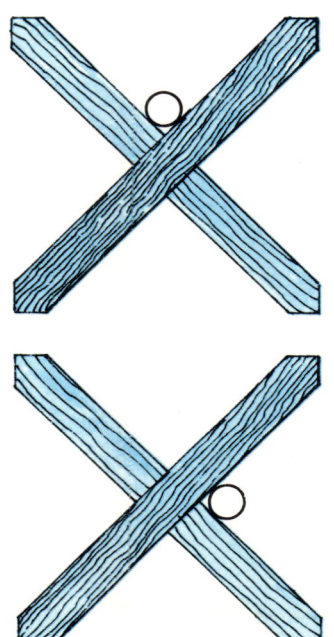

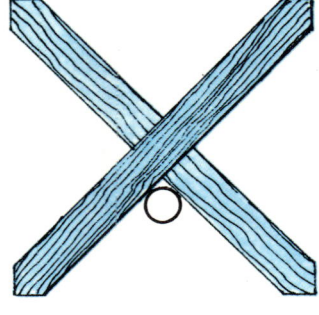

Above & right: cavalletti are most useful pieces of equipment. They are made so that they can be placed at three different heights and they can also be used in various ways to make fences.

The jumping seat involves riding with a slightly shorter stirrup, with your weight carried well forward. You will need, also, to ride with the reins a little shorter than usual. Over small jumps of about 45 cm high the rider does not need to make any exaggerated movement of the body. If the approach is made in the basic jumping position, which will entail the seat being just out of the saddle, all that is necessary is to apply the legs firmly, increasing their pressure in the last three strides and, at the moment of take-off, to push forward with your shoulders and hands. By doing so your seat comes a little more out of the saddle and the forward movement of your shoulders and hands allows the pony to stretch his neck out without any interference with his mouth. As the pony begins to descend from the apex of the jump, the shoulders are straightened and the seat touches down in the saddle once more. Your hands, however, must still allow the pony the freedom of his head.

Below: take-off, flight and landing — three phases of the leap over a cavalletto. Note how the rider has inclined her body forward and is going with the pony who has complete freedom to use his head and neck and to round his back.

Once the pony, and the rider, can cope easily with the little cavalletti fences they can begin to jump proper fences. But again we need to 'hasten slowly' and to introduce the pony to the fence by gradual stages. At all costs we want to avoid a refusal or a run-out, habits which once learnt take time to cure. To start with, we want to build an upright fence against the 'wall' of the school using either three poles, or one pole over a line of drums or something similar. The fence does not need to be more than 60 cm high. To discourage the pony from running out, a 'wing' can be made on the open side by placing a pole from the top of the support to the ground so that it lies almost parallel with the wall.

However, before the actual fence is erected and the pony asked to jump it, put up the supports and the wing and just lay a pole on the ground between the two supports. The pony can then be trotted through the supports and over the pole half a dozen times so that he gets used to the presence of the supports, which he will not have met before. Now the fence can be built properly and a pole laid in front of it. This pole helps the pony to judge the take-off point correctly and its distance from the fence should be the same as the height of the obstacle. Additionally, to help both of you judge the approach and take off it is helpful if you place a cavalletto at lowest height about 10 m in front of the fence. This distance allows two non-jumping strides between landing over the first little obstacle and the point of take off at the second fence. Small ponies, however, will take shorter strides and so in their case the distance will probably be reduced to around 8 m.

The approach should be made at trot and the distance cavalletto jumped from that pace. The pony will then take two canter strides before jumping the principal obstacle. During the approach, the rider squeezes with the legs in time with the stride, giving a firm squeeze to take-off over the first obstacle, followed by three *squeezes*, each stronger than the last, before taking-off over the second fence. In other words: one squeeze on landing over the first, one harder squeeze at the end of the first canter stride and a final, strong squeeze at the end of the next one, which is the signal for the pony to jump. Study the diagram and when actually jumping call out aloud in time with the squeezes – one! two! *three*!

You should, also, teach the pony to jump 'spread' fences. The first one should be a pole 60 cm high with a pole 30 cm in front of it, and one a similar distance behind, both fixed 15 cm lower than the central one to give a spread of 60 cm. Once more the distance fence can be used.

Jump these fences no more than two or three times during one schooling session. Later a fence can be built in the centre of the arena, so that the pony does not become too dependent on the guiding influence of the 'wall' and by gradual stages the wings can be dispensed with.

In jumping a fence like this, ride in front of it, at first in a circle at trot, turning the pony into the fence only when he is calm and balanced. After landing come back to trot and circle again so that the pony does not get into the habit of becoming excited by jumping or rushing his fences.

Until the pony, and the rider, can jump small fences calmly and correctly there is no point in attempting bigger obstacles. It is even more important to realise that until the pony has been made balanced, obedient and supple by the work done on the flat he will never be able to jump successfully. All the horses you see jumping in the big international competitions at Hickstead, Wembley, Aachen or New York spend far more time being schooled on the flat than they ever do jumping fences.

Below: the real thing. Pony and rider jumping in a competition. The steep angle of ascent has made it necessary for the rider to get well forward in order not to be left behind the movement.

Holidays in the Saddle

Holidaying with a pony is one of the best ways to see new countries or new parts of the one in which you live. Basically riding holidays can be divided into two types: the trekking holiday, or the one at a centre where instruction, including jumping, is given daily. The variety of holidays offered is very great. In Britain there are literally hundreds of places to choose from and there are almost as many in the other European countries as well as in such exciting places as Iceland.

Trekking is probably the most popular form of riding holiday, involving daily treks from a centre of upwards of 25 km per day. Most centres give some basic instruction in saddling-up, basic riding and so on, and most encourage holidaymakers to look after a pony, under supervision, during the period of their stay. The majority have residential accommodation, although in many cases this will be in the form of dormitories, and offer a package holiday which includes riding, meals and accommodation. It is possible, however, to find centres where a variety of accommodation away from the establishment can be used, and it is not impossible to stay in an area where there are a number of trekking stables and to book treks on odd days.

Post-trekking differs in that riders start from the centre and stay at different places along the route. Usually such treks are restricted to riders having some experience.

In both instances riders need to be equipped with wet weather gear and generally stout clothes in sufficient quantity. It is always advisable to use a hard hat, otherwise clothes are informal.

Treks are carried out under the control of a trek-leader and the pace, in view of the distances covered and the fact that many trekkers are novice riders, is restricted to walk, trot and the very occasional canter at the discretion of the trek-leader.

Below: an invigorating ride by the sea.

Intending holiday makers are, however, advised to make thorough enquiries before booking a trekking holiday. Accommodation, for instance, varies very considerably and what may suit one will not suit another.

Instructional riding holidays are not quite so numerous but there are still plenty of places to go throughout Europe. Riding will usually be restricted to about two sessions of just over an hour each day, but it will be pretty concentrated stuff and quite enough for most riders. Dress standards are likely to be more formal than at trekking centres and hard hats are certain to be compulsory.

Britain

Trekking centres abound in Scotland, Wales, the West Country, the New Forest area of Hampshire, in Cumbria and in Yorkshire and, indeed, wherever there are stretches of rideable, open country. In each case these are areas of outstanding natural beauty, some of which are National Parks. Usually a cobby type of animal is preferred and in Scotland, the Highland Pony is used extensively. Elsewhere the sort of pony or cob used is usually based on British native pony blood, the Highland, of course, is a recognised British native. In the rest of Europe ponies are not so numerous, although, of course, they exist and many riding centres, such as those in Spain and Portugal, are forced to make use of horses.

Addresses of centres appear regularly in the equestrian magazines: *Horse and Hound*, *Riding*, *Light Horse*, *Pony*, and so on, and advertisements also appear in these papers for centres outside Britain. In general such establishments are reputable and reliable but clearly no magazine is able to check the excellence or otherwise of the places advertised. A very good guide, however, is provided by the Ponies of Britain approval scheme. This society inspects and approves centres on application. It is primarily concerned with the fitness of the animals employed, suitability of saddlery and general supervision but its large list of approved establishments gives full details of accommodation, etcetera, that is available. The list is obtainable from the: Ponies of Britain, Brookside Farm, Ascot, Berks., price 25p, and is well worth studying.

In Britain the law requires every riding establishment to be inspected and registered by its appropriate local authority under the Riding Establishments Act. The act, however, is only concerned with the welfare of the animals, and apart from stipulating supervision of rides is not concerned with other aspects such as accommodation and meals. In theory, the Act should preclude the existence of sub-standard concerns but that, alas, is not always the case. There are bad establishments and for this reason holiday makers are advised to check carefully before booking or to be guided by the Ponies of Britain list.

Schools offering instructional riding holidays are numerous. A booklet, *Where to Ride*, can be obtained from the: British Horse Society, The National Equestrian Centre, Stoneleigh, Warwickshire, for 40p. Schools included in this booklet are

Above: Somerset, where this picture was taken, is one of the loveliest of English counties and there are lots of holidays that can be taken there.

Below: a useful sort.

67

approved under the B.H.S. inspection and approval scheme. Further lists can be obtained from the: Association of British Riding Schools, Chesham House, 56 Green End Road, Sawtry, Huntingdon PE17 5OY, price 25p.

In some cases magazines are able to provide holiday information. *Riding*, for instance, will supply details of holidays in Britain or abroad, or the addresses where information can be obtained, and also holiday information sheets, on specific countries, compiled by its Travel Editor.

The Ponies of Britain list also includes details of Irish centres and a further list can be obtained from: Bord na gCapall, St. Maelrun's, Tallaght, Co. Dublin.

France

This is a country offering great variety for the holiday horseman in almost every part of France from Normandy to the South Pyrenees. The Dordogne is a beautiful area and in the Camargue delta it is possible to ride the famous white horses of the region. At Saumur (Maine-et-Loire department) is the famous school of the Cadre Noir. France, of all the European countries, has the greatest choice of riding holiday and information is available from a number of sources.

The national body concerned with equestrian holidays is Cheval-Voyage, 8 Rue de Milan, Paris 9.

Other useful addresses are: The French Government Tourist Office, 178 Piccadilly, London W1V 0AL; The UCPA, 62 Rue de la Clacière, 75-Paris; Flaine Information Centre, 45a Kensington High Street, London W8; Havas Travel, 21 Connaught Street, Marble Arch, London W2; Club Mediterranée, 17 Hanover Square, London W1R 0AA; Association Départmentale de Tourisme Equestre, 46-Assier (for Quercy region); Association Nationale des Ranchmen de France, Ranch de la Pommeraie, Marsauceux per Mezières en Orduais (The Association of Wild West Ranches).

West Germany

The three principal holiday areas are the Rhineland, the Black Forest and Bavaria and the 'Little Switzerland' in Schleswig-Holstein.

There are some 300 riding establishments in the Federal Republic offering horses for hire, but information is often obtainable only from local tourist offices. It is probably best to contact the German National Tourist Office, which has premises in London at 61 Conduit Street, W1R 0EN. The Tourist Office can supply a useful booklet, *Special Interest Holidays in the Rhineland* and is able to advise on other areas.

Iceland

Riding in Iceland is for those who like adventurous holidays. Although much of the country is sparse and infertile there are areas of incredible beauty and, of course, there are the hot springs, bubbling mud pools and at Geysir is the Great Geysir which has given its name to all such phenomena throughout the world.

Trekking, either by the day or the week, is a well-established holiday feature and the unique Iceland ponies, decandants of those brought to Iceland by the Vikings, make excellent mounts for either beginners or more experienced riders.

One point, though, for intending holiday-makers. If riding breeches or jodhpurs are taken into the country they must be either brand new or have been dry-cleaned and disinfected. It is probably better to wear stout jeans.

Holiday information can be got from: Icelandair, 73 Grosvenor Street, London W1X 9DD; Loftleidir Icelandic Airlines, 45 South Audley Street, London W1; Anglo-Icelandic Travel, 14 High Street, Pinner, Middlesex; Iceland Tourist Information Bureau (same address as Icelandair); Scantours Ltd., 8 Spring Gardens, Trafalgar Square, London SW1; Cooks, 45 Berkeley Street, London W1A.

Below: if you go to Austria you will have the opportunity to see the world-famous Lipizzaner horses in a performance by the Spanish Riding School of Vienna.

Austria

The country is generally mountainous and scattered with lakes with an abundance of interesting wild life. The climate is equable, the hottest months being June to August with temperatures around 70°F. There are some 150 towns and villages where horses can be hired and there are a number of riding schools with varied facilities.

Information can be obtained from the: Osterreichische Campagnereiter-Gesellschaft Bundesfachverband für Reiten und Fahren, Prinz-Eugen Strasse 12, A-1040 Vienna.

Additionally, an excellent booklet, *Equestrian Sports in Austria*, can be obtained from the Austrian National Tourist Offices. In London its address is: 16, Conduit Street, London W1R 0NP. A number of British travel agencies organise riding holidays in Austria, notably Charles Cavendish Ltd., 43 St. George's Walk, Croydon, Surrey CRO 1YL, and Erna Low Travel Service Ltd., 47 Old Brompton Road, London SW7.

A feature of Austria of particular interest to riders is the Spanish Riding School of Vienna, the home of the white Lipizzaner stallions. Tickets for performances, however, must be obtained well in advance.

Belgium

Riding is available throughout the country, particularly in the area of the Ardennes.

Information is obtainable from: The Belgian National Tourist Office (London address: 66 Haymarket, London SW1); Fédération du Tourisme de la Province de Namur, 2a Place de la Gare, Namur, Belgium; Fédération du Tourisme de la Province de Liège, Avenue Blonden, 33 Liège, Belgium.

Among tour operators featuring Belgium is the: Belgian Travel Service Ltd., 63 Ebury Street, London SW1.

Luxembourg

The province of Luxembourg includes the lovely Ardennes towns of Bouillon, St. Hubert and La Roche. Information on riding facilities from: Fédération Touristique du Luxembourg Belge, Clairue 7, La Roche en Ardenne.

Denmark

Denmark may not be so scenically exciting as some countries but it offers a lot of riding holidays with the emphasis on the 'farmhouse' type. There are two large riding centres situated in Jutland, one of which runs a 'Wild West Camp'. Riding facilities also exist on Sealand and on the garden isle of Funen.

The Danish Tourist Board (London address: Sceptre House, Regent Street, London W1R 8PY) will give details and the following British agencies specialise in Danish holidays: DFDS, Mariner House, Pepys Street, London EC3N 4BX; Scantours Ltd., 8 Spring Gardens, Trafalgar Square, London SW1; YHA Travel, 29 John Adam Street, London WC2N 6JE.

Portugal

The main areas in which to ride are around Lisbon and the Algarve, but it can be very hot in mid-summer.

Lisbon has two 'Centros Hipicos' in the city from which horses can be hired. They are the Escola de Equitacao, Rua Alexandre Herculano 39A and Escola de Equitacao Infante de sagres, Estrada da Luz.

The biggest centre in the Algarve is Vilamoura at Praia de Quarteira where horses can be hired by the hour or for the day. There is an indoor school, outdoor arenas and a jumping area.

Holiday information from: The Portuguese National Tourist Office, 20 Lower Regent Street, London SW1Y 4PH; The Travel Club, Station Road, Upminster, Essex; Lusotor SARL – Vilamoura, 139 Park Lane, Mayfair, London W1; The Algarve

Agency, 61 Brompton Road, London SW3; Moratours, 46 Market Place, Reading, Berks. (this company features coach tours visiting famous studs, and so on, and other places of interest to horse lovers).

Spain

This is a large country full of interest for riders and many riding holidays are available. The principal areas are Andalusia, offering wonderful riding country and the magnificent Andalusian horses; the Levante, basically a coastal region; Catalonia, which includes the Costa Brava, and the often overlooked Basque provinces of the Northern Region. In Majorca there are riding facilities at Magaluf, Palma, Formentor, Arenal and C'an Pastilla.

For information contact: The Spanish National Tourist Office, 70 Jermyn Street, London SW1; Swedish-Lloyd Ltd., Marlow House, Lloyd's Avenue, London EC3; Aventura, 5/7 Kingston Hill, Kingston-upon-Thames, Surrey; The Marquis Antonio de Llomelini Tabarca, Alondra Riding Parties, Alora (Malaga), Spain.

Switzerland

There are plenty of riding centres in this lovely country. Riding is available in Grisons, North-East and Central Switzerland, around Lake Geneva, Berne and Bernese Oberland, Valais and Ticino.

A list of suitable schools, etcetera, *Vacations on Horseback* is issued by the Swiss National Tourist Office, Swiss Centre, 1 New Coventry Street, London W1V 3HG. Swissair, Swiss Centre, 3 New Coventry Street, can also be helpful. Ask for the Alpine Highlife brochure which gives details of riding.

Above: riders in Belgium can enjoy long rides over the coastal sand dunes.

Opposite: is a picture of holiday riders in Spain.

Below: Switzerland is a grand place for a riding holiday and has plenty of riding centres.

Horse and Pony Sports

From the time that man first tamed the wild horse, some four thousand years ago, until well after the turn of the century, horses played a significant role in the development of civilisations. The horse in those times was the only means of transport, he was used in large numbers on the battlefields of the world and he had an important part in working the land. But from very early times the horse also provided sport and recreation and when the motor-car and the steam train ousted him from his traditional uses it was these sporting pursuits which ensured the survival of his species. From the earliest times men must have raced horses against each other to prove which was the fastest and racing must, therefore, be regarded as the oldest sport of them all. Today *flat racing* and racing over fences (*steeplechasing*), which came much later, are established sports all over the world. In many countries, particularly on the Continent, in America, Australia and New Zealand, trotting races are almost as popular as the mounted races and attract huge crowds.

Trotting, or racing in harness, is, indeed, a very old sport. At the 25th Olympiad of Ancient Greece in 680 B.C. chariot racing was a principal event and it had been going on long before that.

Just as old is the sport of *hunting* from horseback. The Assyrians, for instance, hunted the lion with spears, and they rode without a saddle! In India the tiger and the wild boar were hunted by mounted men. In time hounds were introduced to the chase, originally pursuing boar and stag. It is this form of hunting which survives today. The stag is still hunted but the most popular form is fox hunting, a sport which started in Britain some three hundred years ago. There are about three hundred packs in the U.K. and Eire hunting the fox as well as some that hunt hares (harriers) and a few more hunting the stag.

Below: the Assyrians were a race of mighty horsemen. This bas-relief shows them hunting the lion from horseback, and they didn't have saddles either! *British Museum, London.*

To many people fox hunting appears to be an elite sport, but, in fact, this is not so. It is extraordinarily democratic and anyone can join in, having once paid his subscription to the hounds, or a 'cap' — a fixed sum asked of visitors for a single day's hunting.

In Britain children who are members of the Pony Club are allowed to hunt for a very nominal figure.

Hunting with hounds, but without a live quarry, i.e. 'drag' hunting, over a prepared line made by dragging an artificial scent (aniseed is often used) over a piece of country, is a later introduction.

There are a few such hunts in Britain and one or two in America, also.

Hunting, in fact, is carried on extensively in America as well as in Australia and New Zealand and also in India and South Africa, where jackal is the quarry. In France there is fox hunting in the Pau region but elsewhere a stylised form of stag hunting is practised.

Competitive sports in what we call the 'three disciplines' of riding are of much more recent origin. These three disciplines are dressage, show jumping and combined training, or simply eventing.

The word 'dressage' means no more than 'training', which is something that men have been doing as long as they have been associated with horses.

Modern dressage is therefore a test of the horse's training and of his obedience to the rider. Dressage competitions at the lowest level, for novice horses, are comparatively simple. The horse is required to carry out elementary movements at walk, trot and canter on either rein, to halt quietly and correctly and possibly to rein back a few paces. Marks are given for each movement in the test and the judges are looking for free, balanced paces, good rhythm throughout and above all for free, forward movement. Resistances to the bit and other disobediences are heavily penalised, as are 'stiff' horses that cannot bend their bodies in the direction of the movement.

As the training of the horse progresses the tests become more demanding. Better balance is required, a higher head carriage and more advanced movements, such as half-pass

Below: Britain has a unique school of sporting art, one of its greatest exponents being Henry Alken who painted this exciting picture. *Sotheby's, London.*

(moving laterally) and the counter canter, in which the horse has to prove his obedience and balance by cantering a circle on 'the wrong leg', i.e. the right fore leading on a circle left.

The majority of well-made horses are quite able to perform tests up to an intermediate standard and dressage to this level should be a part of every riding horse's education. Such training develops his muscles and gymnastic ability, makes him obedient, easy and balanced in his paces and, as a result, a pleasure to ride.

Beyond this point, however, dressage becomes an end in itself and also an art. The highest level of dressage test is the Olympic Grand Prix and this involves many highly collected movements which are not entirely relevant to the ordinary riding horse. Movements are asked for in each gait at the ordinary pace, the working one, the extended and the collected and include such advanced work as the changes of leg at canter, in one, two or three time; the pirouettes at canter and the spectacular collected movements of *passage* (when the horse advances slowly with an elevated action) and *piaffe* (when he marks time on the spot).

The greatest and best-known exponents of the art of dressage are the riders of the famous 400-year-old Spanish Riding School in Vienna. There, however, you can see the 'airs' or leaps above the ground, *capriole*, *ballotade* and so on which are part of haute école riding and not included in dressage tests. These movements are thought to be those practised by the armoured knights in battle to strike terror into their enemies and to scatter any surrounding foot soldiers.

Below: a good picture of a pony and rider in action over a big fence at the All-England Jumping Arena at Hickstead.

Dressage as a sport is practised all over the world but there is no doubt that the continental European nations, particularly the Germans, are the leaders in this field, due to their tradition of indoor, school riding. In Britain, on the other hand, the equestrian tradition is firmly based on the hunting field, and as a result there are not nearly so many advanced dressage riders in the country in comparison with Britain's neighbours over the Channel.

Dressage, using the word in the sense of high school riding, has been practised ever since the days of the first Master, the Greek general, Xenophon (circa 430–350 B.C.), and during the Renaissance period kings and noblemen displayed their skills in hundreds of Baroque riding halls throughout Europe. Show jumping, however, the second of our disciplines, is a very recent sport in comparison, only beginning at the very end of the last century. It is, indeed, only over the past twenty-five years that it has achieved its present popularity.

It is, of course, an entirely artificial sport, although an exciting one, with horses jumping a course of made-up, coloured fences. These fences, basically, are of three types: uprights, parallels, or spread, fences and 'staircases', which also involve a spread. But there can be many variations on these themes: walls, stiles, oxers, crossed poles without a ground line and so on. In recent years natural obstacles have been introduced into the big arenas, like Hickstead and Hamburg, notably the big banks. The fences themselves present problems, depending on their shape, height and

Below: this is a riding club team about to perform a quadrille with a circus theme. Look how beautifully the horses have been turned out.

spread, the existence or otherwise of a ground line, and, in outside arenas, on the position of the fences in relation to the fall or otherwise of the ground.

In International competitions fences may be upwards of 1·5 m with corresponding spreads, though in novice competitions fences are much lower and each will have a distinct ground line. In both, however, the layout or track, together with the distances between fences, causes equal problems.

Two or more fences, for instance, can be placed to follow directly after each other and if the inside distance between any two is not more than 12 m then it is termed a combination and is usually numbered as one obstacle.

Easy distances allowing for one and two non-jumping strides between fences are 7 m and 10 m approximately, but if these are made either greater or smaller a half-stride will be involved and the problem becomes a difficult one demanding a supple, obedient horse who will either lengthen or shorten, according to the indications given by his rider, so that he arrives at the take-off point for the second part of the combination correctly.

These distances have to be altered if the two fences of a combination are of different types, i.e. parallel and upright. In this case the distance must be increased as the horse will have to jump the first faster and consequently will land further out. For the opposite arrangement the distance must be shortened, otherwise the horse will be forced to 'reach' for the second fence.

A combination of two fences is called a 'double' and of three, a 'treble'.

The universal rules of show jumping award 4 faults for a knock down, 3 for a first refusal, 6 for a second and elimination for a third. A fall of horse and rider, or of the rider alone, is penalised 8 faults.

Basically there are six main forms of competition: **1.** A1 in which competitors, if still equal after two jump offs divide the prize money; **2.** A2 in which riders jump against the clock in the second jump off, the fastest time with the least faults winning; **3.** A3 in which the clock is used in the same way in the first jump off; **4.** A4 pure speed competitions in which the clock is used on the first round, the winner being the rider with the fastest time and the least number of faults; **5.** timed competitions in which 6–10 seconds are added to the total time taken for each fence knocked down. Examples are Take Your Own Line, Scurry and Pair Relay competititions. **6.** Competitions such as Hit and Hurry, Accumulator, Have a Gamble, etc., which have their own special rules.

In speed competititions fences are always lower than otherwise.

Before any competitition, riders are allowed to 'walk the course'. This gives them an opportunity to plan their approach to the course and the line they think best to take, as well as to pace out the distances between combinations. Style is never taken into account. Horses and riders can jump as they please, but it is usually the well-trained horse and rider, jumping correctly, that wins.

Above: one of the most famous of equestrian portraits is this one of Charles I painted by Van Dyck. The King, who was an accomplished horseman is riding an Andalucian stallion which, up until the 18th century, was regarded as the first horse of Europe. *National Gallery, London.*

Below: this very beautiful picture by Gozzoli is called *The Journey of the Magi*. This Italian artist painted his figures in the clothing of his time but as it is an allegorical scene it is not a strictly accurate depiction. However it is a wonderfully active painting of man and horse. *Riccardi Palace, Florence.*

The sport of *combined training* had its origin in what used to be known as 'The Military', a competition based on the role of the horseman in war. The idea, at its roots, was that of the aide carrying despatches across open country, negotiating natural obstacles as he came to them. With this in mind a competition evolved which commenced with a dressage test, to prove the suppleness, obedience and suitability of the horse, followed by a cross-country course. Eventually, to prove that after his exertions the horse was still fit for service, a jumping phase was introduced.

Today there are three distinct types of combined training competition. *Combined competititions* comprise tests in dressage and jumping; *horse trials* comprise dressage, jumping and cross-country; *three-day events*, like those at Badminton, Burghley and at the Olympics, are made up of a dressage test, a speed, endurance and cross-country phase, which may involve as much as 27 km and includes roads and tracks, a steeplechase course and the final cross-country of about 7 km over as many as 30 obstacles, and then on the final day a test of jumping.

Such a competition is the ultimate test of the bold and well-schooled horse and horseman and is arguably the toughest of all sports.

Judging is fairly complicated with each competitor's marks being carried forward in the form of penalties from the first day to the last.

The marking is very much different from show jumping. Time is involved in the speed, endurance and cross-country phase and, indeed, also in the jumping test, penalties being awarded for time taken exceeding the maximum allowed. In the former the time allowed is tight and competitors must go a fair pace all the way if they are to avoid penalties. As fences are fixed on the steeplechase and cross-country phases, knockdowns do not occur, but 20 penalties are awarded for a refusal, 40 for a second at the same obstacle and elimination for a third at the same obstacle. Sixty penalties are exacted for falls, which in three-day events can be fairly numerous, and three falls on the course results in elimination. In the final jumping phase over coloured show jumps a knockdown constitutes 10 penalties, a first refusal 10 and a second on the course 20. A fall costs 30 penalties.

Fences on a three-day event course can be spectacular. They are always formidable and sometimes horrific. At Badminton there are banks, walls, obstacles in and out of lanes, water and always a variety of problem obstacles which can be jumped in a number of ways. Many of these huge fences have to be jumped either up or down hill and one of the former at the end of the course and on a tired horse represents a real difficulty.

A near relation of combined training is the *hunter trial*, originally conceived as a test for hunters but today, in Britain, more often looked on as a good school for a potential eventer. The hunter trial is a test over a cross-country course but, in the event of a number of clear rounds it is usually the fastest time that wins.

Above & below: one of the world's fastest games is polo and it calls for a fast, agile pony and a good horseman.

Showing horses at the big horse and agricultural shows is not such a dangerous undertaking. The purpose of the horse show classes, for hunters, cobs, ponies, hacks and harness turnouts, is to find the 'perfect' stamp or type of horse for a particular purpose, or in the case of breed classes, such as those confined to native ponies or Arabs, to find the 'perfect' specimen of the particular breed. In this way it is hoped to encourage the breeding of only the best. In Britain show classes do not involve any proof of performance, beyond walking, trotting, cantering and galloping, apart from the 'working' classes for hunters and hunter ponies which are partially judged on jumping ability over a small course of natural fences. In America, however, performance classes are very much the thing and great emphasis is laid on jumping and doing so in the correct style.

Many shows put on classes which cater for the more run-of-the-mill animals, the riding horses, handy and family ponies, and so on, and in Britain there are literally thousands of gymkhana shows.

The *gymkhana*, or mounted games, comprises all sorts of events: bending races, potato races, musical sacks and so on. They provide a first-class competititive outlet for children with ordinary ponies that may not be good enough to show or to take part in serious jumping events.

Increasingly, *driving* is becoming more and more popular and indeed this aspect of horse sports is almost a world on its own. Horses can be driven singly, in pairs, in tandem (one in front of the other) and as a team of four to something like a road coach. Apart from competing at shows, taking part in driving rallies and so on, there are ride and drive competitions for the enthusiast and even a three-day driving event which follows the pattern of the mounted one but, of course, without the jumps.

Long-distance or endurance riding is yet another outlet for the horseman. Rides may vary from 30 to 120 km or more and have to be covered at certain set speeds. No jumping is involved but the sport demands a highly conditioned horse that will remain sound throughout to pass the stringent veterinary checks, and a fit rider who can adjust the pace to suit the country whilst keeping to the required speed. No racing element is involved in endurance riding and no extra marks are gained for completing the course in under the time set.

Finally, there is the game of *polo*, brought to Europe in the nineteenth century by British officers who had learnt the game in India. Polo, for teams of four players, is well named the galloping game. The ponies need to be fast and very agile for they must turn on a penny to follow the play of the ball. The players as well as being competent horsemen have to be good at ball games. To hit a ball accurately from a fast-galloping pony requires a good eye and lots of practice, too.

In fact there is a horse sport for everyone who owns or rides a horse or pony, and if none of them appeals there is always the pleasure of hacking quietly through the countryside in an altogether satisfying partnership.